CLIFF BASTIN REMEMBERS

THE AUTOBIOGRAPHY OF ARSENAL'S
GREATEST OUTSIDE-LEFT

In collaboration with

BRIAN GLANVILLE

GCR BOOKS LIMITED
www.gcrbooks.co.uk

With thanks to
PATRICIA VICARY & BARBARA LAMBERT
for their generosity and kind
cooperation in the
republication of their father's book.

Special thanks also to
BRIAN GLANVILLE
for his consent and support for this project.

First Published in Great Britain 1950 by The Ettrick Press, London.

This edition published 2010 by GCR Books Ltd.
Registered in England & Wales. Reg No. 6949535
www.gcrbooks.co.uk
ISBN 978-0-9559211-4-8

Copyright © Cliff Bastin & Brian Glanville 1950

Text and editing by GCR Books Ltd
Cover image © Patricia Vicary and Barbara Lambert

All rights reserved. No reproduction, copy or transmission of this publication may be made without written permission or in accordance with the provisions of the Copyright, Design and Patents Act 1988 (as amended). Any person who does any unauthorized act in relation to this publication may be liable to criminal prosecution and civil claims for damages.

This book is sold subject to the condition that it shall not, by way of trade or otherwise, be lent, resold, hired out, or otherwise circulated without the publisher's prior consent in any form of binding or cover other than that in which it was published and without a similar condition including this condition being imposed on the subsequent purchaser.

Printed and bound in Great Britain by CPI

FOREWORD

During the various eras of football many professional players come and go, and when their careers are finished on the field a few names remain which are never forgotten in the years that follow. It is true to say that in the football world these particular names live among the immortals, and Clifford Sidney Bastin, to my mind, earned the right to this niche in football history which nobody will deny.

I was more fortunate than most people in the fact that practically the whole of Clifford Bastin's career coincided with my own behind-the-scenes activities. I have always stated and have always believed through my own experience that the greater the player the less trouble he causes to the people who have to deal with the management of his career. Cliff was certainly a very true illustration of this point, and I could sum up his character briefly in saying that his sincerity, his gratitude and his loyalty to his club and "bosses" were something that really could be a pattern for any youthful footballers or any matured footballers to use as an example. Coupled to this, he had a trait in his character which few of us are blessed with – that is, he had an ice-cold temperament.

No matter how big the occasion, no matter what sudden success was thrust upon him, his mental attitude was never unbalanced; in fact I would say the greater the occasion the more cool and accurate did Cliff become in his efforts on the field of play.

I look on this as a great honour to have the privilege of paying this tribute to one of the names in football which, as I said, will remain immortal, and also to a man who has been a great friend and epitomises the word "gentleman" on and off the field of football.

Tom Whittaker, M.B.E.
September 1950

CONTENTS

Chapter		Pages
1.	SCHOOLBOY FOOTBALL	1
2.	I JOIN EXETER AND AM TRANSFERRED TO ARSENAL	6
3.	MY FIRST GAMES FOR ARSENAL	13
4.	THE ROAD TO WEMBLEY	19
5.	WE WIN THE F.A. CUP	25
6.	OUR RECORD SEASON	41
7.	MY FIRST INTERNATIONAL	48
8.	WE FALL BETWEEN TWO STALLS	54
9.	THE GREATNESS OF TOM WHITTAKER	60
10.	WHO WAS WHO AT HIGHBURY	69
11.	MY PARTNERSHIP WITH ALEX JAMES	86
12.	THAT WALSALL AFFAIR	89
13.	ROLL ON, THE GUNNERS!	94
14.	THE CHANGING SCENE AT HIGHBURY	99
15.	ABROAD WITH ENGLAND	106
16.	WE WIN THE CUP AGAIN	121
17.	THE SCENE CHANGES AGAIN	125
18.	PERSONALITIES I KNEW	133
19.	MY LAST TOUR	139
20.	MARS INTERVENES	144
21.	BLINDMAN'S BUFF AT TOTTENHAM	164
22.	MY LAST GAME FOR ARSENAL	173
23.	HINTS FOR THE YOUNG ENTHUSIAST	178
24.	FOOTBALL TODAY – AND TOMORROW	186
25.	IN RETROSPECT	194

1
SCHOOLBOY FOOTBALL

Almost as soon as I could walk, I was kicking a football. Just why the bug got into my boots so early, I'm afraid I cannot say. My father could hardly tell the difference between a goal and a goalpost, and it was only when I was at quite an advanced stage in my soccer career that he began to take any interest in the game at all.

Be that as it may, it has always held a fascination for me, and at the age of nine I made my first appearance for my school: Ladysmith Road School, Exeter. This was in 1921, and was my only game for them that year. Curiously enough, I played in the outside-left position; where of course I was to settle down in future years with Arsenal. This may not seem remarkable at first, but in actual fact I don't think I had another game on the left wing until nine years later, with Arsenal!

A second coincidence was that the Ladysmith Road colours were red and white, as, of course, are Arsenal's! Perhaps my subsequent career was preordained, had I only known it!

The following year I gained a regular place in the school team, at inside-left, and, under the able and kindly guidance of Mr. Yeoman, the master who looked after the sporting side of our education, began to find my feet.

It is impossible for me to assess fully the debt I owe to Mr. Yeoman; nor can I thank him enough for the kindly interest he took in me, throughout the time I was at Ladysmith Road. He was always ready with encouragement and sound advice, and it was only an inadequate expression of my gratitude when I sent him my winners' medal, after the Cup Final of 1930. Had it not been for him, it is more than probable that I should never have been in a position to win it.

In this, my first season as a regular in the Ladysmith Road team, we were called upon to defend the Devon Shield which we had won the year before. The competition for this shield took place towards the end of every season, between the leading school teams of every town and city throughout Devon. In other words, you had to win your local league in order to qualify.

This particular year, we got through the earlier rounds quite comfortably, but the semi-final provides me with a memory which rivals any experience I had with Arsenal or even England.

We were drawn against Tiverton School, and the first game, at Exeter, ended all square. For the second game – played at Tiverton – the referee appeared in a red and white football jersey, and white shorts! This in itself was bad enough, but to make matters worse, red and white were, as I have mentioned, our own colours! Mr. Yeoman tried to make the tactless official listen to reason, but it was all of no avail. He turned out just as he was! I couldn't believe my eyes, and I must admit that I spent most of the game gazing at him with mingled astonishment and admiration! If I had only been a little older, I might have said to myself, "Solomon in all his glory was not arrayed like one of these!"

We drew that game, too, but it was in the third, played on a neutral ground, that the trouble started. The referee in charge was stoned by the Tiverton supporters, and had the back of his head cut open as he left the field, at the end of another drawn game.

The fourth game was played at Exminster, behind closed doors, the only time this has happened in my experience. We went on to retain the shield. We won it the next four years, too.

Those days of schoolboy football were very happy ones for me. I honestly think I enjoyed them more than I did my career in top-grade football, and I hope readers will bear with me if I bring back one or two more reminiscences of them.

The most exciting game I have ever played in – and I'm not forgetting the F.A. Cup semi-final against Hull, in 1930, when I equalised for Arsenal, a couple of minutes from time – was against the Bluecoat School, Barnstable, in 1925. This too was a semi-final – the semi-final of the Devon Shield. Ladysmith Road were a goal down, with only eight minutes left to play, and Mr. Yeoman was pacing frantically up and down the touch-line, lighting one cigarette after another, only to throw each away, after a couple of puffs!

Then I scored twice in three minutes, when all seemed lost, and we eventually added a third, for a 3-1 victory. An unimportant match, perhaps, but it is one I shall always remember!

I played a number of games for the Exeter Schools side, in the English Shield, too, but we were never quite so successful. The early rounds were "zoned", and, sooner or later, we always had to meet Bristol – and we always lost! It was in one of these games that I played myself into an England trial (schoolboy, of course!), but more of that in its proper place.

The start of the matter was when Mr. Yeoman decided that I was worthy of international recognition. I was fourteen years old at the time, by the way. Accordingly, he wrote to the English schools selectors, giving them full details of my football career to date – the representative appearances I had made, the number of goals I had scored, and practically everything else he could think of, which was remotely relevant. It was more of a book, than a letter! Without it, I would never have come to the notice of the selectors, for they never looked as far afield as the West Country when picking their teams.

The upshot of Mr. Yeoman's activity was that one of the selection committee, Mr. Crandon, watched me in the Bristol v Exeter English Schools' Shield game, at Bristol, to find out whether I was worthy of a trial. And he nearly didn't see me! On the way up in the train, I suffered from a severe bilious attack. I played, however, although I felt so ill that it was just about the last thing I wanted to do.

The pitch was waterlogged, and the game was played ankle-deep in mud. These conditions effectively disposed of any chance we might have had of winning this tie. The Bristol boys – who, by the way, included Ronnie Dix, later to make his name with more clubs than I care to remember – were a far bigger and heavier side than ourselves.

We lost that game, but, curiously enough, I had a good match. As I have said, I felt thoroughly ill, but I have often noticed that I have touched my best form on occasions when I would rather have been in a sick-bed. However, my prevailing reaction when I came off the field was one of bitter disappointment. Bristol, had proved too good for us yet again.

But there was a silver lining in this cloud. Mr. Crandon was impressed by my display, and I was selected to play for the Southern Schools in their international trial match against the Midlands. I did well enough in this game to be selected for the final trial, North v South, in which I think I played just about as well as I possibly could have done.

After the game, the players on both sides sat down to a high tea, during which the team to meet Scotland, at Sunderland, was to be announced. When, after what seemed an age, the Chairman of the selection committee stood up to read out the names of the lucky ones among us, I held my breath with excitement and apprehension. At last, it came to my position – inside-left. I could hardly have played any better – it must be me! One brief syllable was enough to wreck my hopes. "Smith" was the name the Chairman read out.

Mr. Yeoman was quite as disappointed as I was. I had been chosen as a reserve, however, and he told me that my time was sure to come. Smith, he explained, was a Sunderland boy, and since the match was taking place in his own town, the selectors had decided to include him: even if I had played like a superman. I still could not have won my way into the team. Smith, incidentally, was Septimus Smith, later to have such a distinguished career with Leicester City.

England won the International against Scotland 3-0, and Sep Smith had quite a good match. Yet he was dropped for the next game, against Wales, and I was put in his place. This was proof positive that the selectors had chosen him simply because they thought that the appearance of a local boy in the England team would swell the gate. There was no excuse for dropping him had he been chosen on merit alone, for, as I have remarked, his display was entirely satisfactory. It was a bad and unfair system, this "boys for grounds" idea, and I sincerely hope it is no longer practised in schools' Soccer today.

Naturally I was overjoyed at being awarded my international cap, and I grudged almost every second of the days which stood between me and the game at Aberdare. Yet when the great day came, I was almost balked of my ambition. It happened like this.

For some reason best known to the English and Welsh selectors, the players on both sides were required to produce their birth certificates, immediately before the game. Why the certificates couldn't have been produced during the several weeks which came between the announcement of the team and the game itself, I really cannot say. However, the point was that they did have to be produced, and, on arrival at the ground, horror of horrors, Mr. Yeoman had left mine behind!

I need hardly tell you what frantic telegraphing and telephoning ensued! Mr. Yeoman wired home to his wife – she couldn't find it! But at last when it seemed that red tape was going to deprive me of an international cap, the wretched certificate turned up, and I played.

We won, 2-1, and I scored one of the goals. I must have had a good game; although the only impression I had after the match was that I enjoyed myself; for many of the spectators congratulated me, when I was coming away from the ground. I was even told by one man, in future years, that the goal which I scored that day was the best that he had ever seen; but whether he was joking or not, I don't really know.

My partner at inside-forward that day was Len Goulden, later to make up the left-wing pair with me in full internationals. Sid Cann and Leslie Howe, who subsequently joined Manchester City and Tottenham Hotspur respectively, were other colleagues that day who later made a name for themselves in professional football. Sid now manages Southampton.

That 1926 season was my greatest in schoolboy football. The following year I was too old to qualify for county or international games, or even for the Devon Shield. I consoled myself by scoring over a hundred goals from the centre-half position!

The same year, I signed amateur forms for Exeter City.

2
I JOIN EXETER AND AM TRANSFERRED TO ARSENAL

For some time before I left school there had been an understanding between Exeter City and myself that I should join them when I eventually did leave. Accordingly, they signed me on amateur forms. As I was then only fifteen years old it was, of course, impossible for me to become a professional as yet. Incidentally, it was by no means inevitable that I should have taken up a soccer career. While at Ladysmith Road I had also been a keen cricketer, batting and bowling left-handed with some success. Indeed, Mr. Yeoman often told me that he considered me better at the summer game than I was at football, and strongly advised me to seek a trial with the Devon cricket side. But for me, soccer always came first, and I was glad to accept Exeter's proposal.

It was not until the 1928 season that I gained a regular place in the Exeter City Third Division side, although I played my first game for them towards the end of the previous season, when I was only fifteen years old.

Meanwhile, Exeter would have liked me to turn out regularly for their Reserve team, but the prospect did not attract me particularly. Instead, I made it quite clear to the Exeter City people that the mere fact that I trained a couple of nights a week on their ground, and that they had my signature on amateur forms, did not entitle them to compel me to play for one of their sides.

Consequently, although I did play a number of games for their second string, most of my football in the year or so after leaving school was with St. Mark's, in the Bible Class League, and St. James', in the Second Division of the East Devon League. I enjoyed myself thoroughly with both these teams.

While I was with St. Mark's we won the Bible Class League, and might have won the Cup as well, had I not missed a penalty in the final! While playing with St. James', I gained several County caps for Devonshire, but although we were successful in the earlier rounds of the Southern Counties Championship, we did not manage to go very far in it.

My refusal to take the plunge into the Exeter Reserve side at such an early age was probably the wisest move I made during my soccer career. It meant that instead of spending my Saturday afternoons bouncing off the shoulders of one hefty defender after another, I was gradually building up my strength in grades of football which were not hopelessly far above the schoolboy stuff to which I had been accustomed, while at the same time I was developing and maintaining my own particular style of play.

So many youngsters are persuaded to take part in professional or first-class amateur football long before they have the physical capacity for it. The inevitable result is that all their individualism is almost literally knocked out of them, and they relapse into the limbo of mediocrity. Thus, my advice to all young would-be stars is: don't rush at your objective! Take your time: build your strength and improve your style – then wait for the scouts to come clustering around your front door!

This must seem very queer advice for me to give, when it is remembered that I was the youngest player ever to play in a winning F.A. Cup Final team, and am still remembered as "Boy" Bastin. But this policy of "hastening slowly" was, in my opinion, the most decisive factor in my rapid climb to the top. I only began that climb when I felt that I was fully ready.

Naturally, Exeter City were not quite so happy about the policy I was pursuing as I was myself. They had received strong competition from Blackburn Rovers for my signature, and probably thought I was merely making use of the facilities they could afford me, before deciding to sign for some other club! In actual fact, I had no intention of leaving Exeter for some time to come, and was satisfied at the prospect of playing for the local team on the St. James' ground, where I had played so many representative matches during my school days, and where the City had spotted me.

At the beginning of the 1928-29 season I thought I was ready for the Third Division, and set Exeter City's doubts at rest by informing them of the fact, and turning out regularly for their first team. As I have said before, my appearances in the City Reserves had been, to say the least of it, spasmodic. I remember particularly one occasion when I badly wanted to play for St. James' in a local cup-tie. Accordingly, I persuaded City to rest me that week.

All might easily have gone well, but I scored five times in St. James' 7-1 cup-tie victory, and the fact was reported in the local Press! The next time I turned up for training at the City ground I was greeted by an official with the sardonic remark, "I thought you said you wanted a rest!"

I was still under seventeen years of age, so for the first half of that season I had to play for the City on an amateur basis, as, of course, I had been doing before.

I would like to be able to say that my memories of Exeter City are all happy ones, but I am afraid that this is not so. It is said that money is the root of all evil, so perhaps it is significant that all went well between City and myself until I had turned seventeen, and the time came for me to talk over professional terms with them.

Mr. Syd Thomas, then the club secretary, called me into his office and handed me a pen. There were my professional forms on his desk. All I had to do was sign them. But I was not going to sign those forms blindly, trusting on the City's latent goodness of heart for my future well-being. I read the contract through, and saw that I was to be paid £4 for first team appearances and a pound less for matches in the reserves.

"This is no good to me!" I said.

Mr. Thomas' astonishment was almost painful to behold. "What do you mean?" he snapped.

I pointed out to him that, as a first-year professional, I was entitled to a maximum wage of £5 a week, all the year round, and that unless I received it I had no intention of signing for Exeter.

This somewhat annoyed Mr. Thomas, and in the course of the next few minutes I was afforded the interesting information that I was suffering from a swollen head, and that I would not be given such a salary, even by a First Division club.

I waited until Mr. Thomas had finished his little peroration, then gently informed him that it was all the same to me whether I signed for his club or not, and that if the City thought that I was worth signing on as a professional, I was worth a decent wage as well. Ultimately, Mr. Thomas promised to put the matter to the directors, but told me they were bound to refuse my request.

A rather interesting and amusing incident followed a few days after this interview. Before recounting it, however, I think that I should point out that in those days – matters may have changed since – Exeter City was run by the directors and the secretary. The manager was little more than a figurehead.

At this particular period, that position was filled by Mr. Wilson, and on my return to the dressing-room, after a morning's training, I found him there, too. We walked down to the town together, and he wished me the best of luck in my future career. "As for wages, Cliff," he added, "there's no need to worry about them. You may not be getting your maximum yet, but you soon will be."

Now, I had been informed several days previously that the directors, out of their boundless generosity, had acceded to my request for a maximum wage. Thus, Mr. Wilson's well-meant encouragement simply added up to the fact that he knew nothing about the negotiations over my wages at all. A fine position for a manager to be in!

Although I was playing in Third Division football at such an early age, I must confess that I found it somewhat uninspiring. There was, of course, a great deal more beef and brawn than I had yet been accustomed to, but I considered that there had been quite as much, if not more, skill in schoolboy representative football as there was in the Third Division South.

However, my days with Exeter were numbered.

On a spring afternoon in 1929 I was working in the pump-yard of a farm, with an electrical engineer to whom Exeter City had apprenticed me, as soon as I had left school, when my employer suddenly arrived, and told me to put my coat on.

I did so, clambered into his car, and we drove off. He told me we were going into Exeter, then relapsed into silence, for a few minutes. Suddenly he asked me, "How would you like to sign for Arsenal?" This was something of a surprise to me, to say the least of it, and consequently I felt in no position to give him an answer. But the question was soon to be put rather more forcibly.

On arrival in Exeter, we drove to the offices of a firm of solicitors, Dunn and Baker, where Mr. Thomas, the club secretary, was then employed. Note the significance of this. The procedure of most clubs is to carry on transfer negotiations in the manager's office, or the boardroom. But not Exeter City!

Besides Mr. Thomas, and several other City representatives, the room to which I was shown contained a man with whom I was unacquainted. Plump, rubicund and genial, he was introduced to me by the Exeter officials as Mr. Herbert Chapman, Manager of Arsenal F.C.

There was an aura of greatness about Chapman. I was impressed by him straight away. He possessed a cheery self-confidence, which communicated itself to those around him. This power of inspiration and the remarkable gift of foresight, which never seemed to desert him, were his greatest attributes. From a struggling professional footballer, he fought his way up to become the Napoleon of soccer. I think his qualities were worthy of an even better reward. He should have been Prime Minister, and might have been, had it not been for the restrictions and lack of opportunities entailed by his position in the social scale. Still, everything happens for the best, in this best of all possible worlds (or does it?), and maybe it was better that Chapman should have become pilot of the destinies of a football club, rather than those of a country struggling desperately for economic and political security, in the tragic years between the two World Wars.

I apologise for my digression, but one does not often meet, or, when met, easily forget, such a personality as Herbert Chapman.

Yet for all his imposing presence, and formidable persuasive powers, his invitation for me to join Arsenal failed to inspire me. Financially, there was nothing to be gained by doing so. I was still in my first year as a professional, and although Arsenal would be able to give me a rise the following season, I would miss the benefit money which I should accrue, were I to remain with Exeter City a little longer.

Besides, it must be remembered that Arsenal were not yet the power they were destined to become, although they had been runners-up for the League Championship in 1925-26 and had been beaten in the Cup Final a year later.

Mr. Chapman did all he could to change my mind, and received sterling support from the Exeter party, whose members were obviously entertaining roseate visions of a nice, fat cheque. Besides, the prospect of escaping the payment of my benefit could not have acted as a deterrent to them!

But I was not to be persuaded. I could see very little to be gained by joining Arsenal, while I did not want to leave Exeter – the town, not the club – for some time yet. Remember, I was only seventeen.

The upshot of it was that I left the offices of Dunn and Baker still an Exeter player, and contemplating no change in my status for quite a while to come. But I did not know Chapman!

That evening, he arrived on the front doorstep of my home. I was not particularly pleased to see him. I was due to take part in a competition at the local tennis club in a quarter of an hour or so, and wanted to arrive on time, so that I could play my game before the light faded.

Mr. Chapman, however, had other ideas. He sat himself down at the dining-room table, and began to paint a glowing word-picture of the opportunities that awaited me in London, and, more particularly, at Highbury. He cast me in the role of a sort of footballing Dick Whittington, and took down the vases from the mantelpiece to represent my stepping-stones to fame!

But I remained unimpressed. Frankly, the prospect of signing for Arsenal failed to elicit the smallest amount of enthusiasm from me. I do not want my readers to gather from this that I was an over-confident and absurdly ambitious young man. This was not so at all, in spite of the remarks of the Exeter City secretary, a few months previously!

The fact is that I am, and always have been, essentially phlegmatic in temperament. I am not easily elated; and I am not easily depressed. If Chapman had offered me £10,000 down, an immediate position in the England team, and a half share in the Kimberley diamond mines, I would still have remained quite unexcited. In all honesty, my thoughts were not upon Mr. Chapman's polished and incisive oratory at all. It slipped off me like water off a duck's back. The consideration which remained uppermost in my mind throughout this conversation was whether I should have time at the end of it to play off my tie in the tennis competition!

The shadows were beginning to fall, the lights were going on in the near-by houses, and still there was no break in Chapman's eloquence. I must have had visions of a lifetime spent in listening to him. Anyway, I at last consented to sign, if my mother would agree to it.

We called her in, and asked her what her decision was. She answered immediately, "I've never stood in your way, Cliff. Do just as you please."

This attitude was typical of her. I owe more to her than to anybody else in the world, and shall always be grateful for her kindness and generosity to me. Ours was far from being a rich family. My father earned a very moderate wage, and it was only in future years that I was fully able to appreciate all that my mother did for me, so that I was always as well situated and well provided for as any of my school friends.

Every season, I had a new pair of football books – and a good pair, too. Every time I played in an away match, throughout the years I was at school, I always had money to spend, and when I represented England in a Schoolboy International, I wore a brand-new suit for the occasion.

All this was Mother's doing. How she accomplished it, I still don't know. Her scheming and economy must have been prodigious, and I am sure she often drew on her meagre savings, in order to provide me with the luxuries which made my young life worth living, but which she could ill afford.

Besides, had it not been for her encouragement when I decided to adopt football as a career, it was probable that I should never have entered upon it. Certainly, in this particular instance, it was her words, rather than the Chapman magic, which finally swayed me to sign the form which the Arsenal Manager flourished in front of me.

As soon as I had done this, I hurried off to the tennis courts, still hoping to get my game. "Sorry I'm late," I said to my friends, when I arrived there. "I've just been signing for Arsenal." I said these words in a matter-of-fact tone, and this tone was absolutely genuine. I had been none too keen on signing, and now that I had signed, I felt quite indifferent about it.

My friends, however, wouldn't believe me. "You're kidding!" they said. Ultimately, I convinced them that I was in earnest, whereupon they seemed much more excited about the matter than I was myself!

I have sometimes wondered whether this phlegmatic temperament of mine has not deprived me of a great deal of enjoyment, as represented by the elation I should have felt on occasions, had I been of a more excitable nature. Perhaps it has. Nevertheless, I think, all things considered, it has been an advantage to me: since it was the basis of one of the most important qualities which went to make my soccer career a success: the ability to keep a cool head whatever the circumstances.

Yet as I lay in bed that night, waiting for sleep to come, the prospect of London rose before my eyes, and even I was a trifle impressed!

3
MY FIRST GAMES FOR ARSENAL

Although I may not have any outstanding memories of my association with the Exeter football team, the townspeople have made sure that I shall never forget the city of my birth and boyhood. Several years after I had joined Arsenal, when I had achieved international status, they decided to make a presentation to me. The day of that presentation was one of the proudest and happiest in my life.

Accompanied by Mr. Herbert Chapman, who had lured me away from Devon, and by Sir Samuel Hill-Wood, the Chairman of the Arsenal Board of Directors, I journeyed down to Exeter, to receive two fine gifts from the Mayor, on behalf of the good folk of the town.

The more important of the two was a splendid polished wooden cabinet, specially designed to hold my caps and medals. But this was not all. I also received my portrait in oils, in which I am wearing my England colours, painted by Mr. Henry Whykes. But I am jumping ahead of my subject.

Shortly before I was due to report at Highbury, to begin training for the new season, my grandmother was taken gravely ill, and I was given permission to delay my departure for London. Grandmother died before I left Exeter, and among her last words to me was a warning which she had given me countless times before.

"Don't ever go to London, Cliff!" she said. To her, the capital city was nothing but Sodom or Gomorrah, full of snares and pitfalls for innocent young West Country lads, such as myself! Grandmother undoubtedly warned me in what she considered to be my best interests, but on the whole, I am glad I did not heed her advice!

I travelled to London a week after the rest of the Arsenal players had reported back for training. This meant that I missed the pre-season pep-talks which Herbert Chapman always gave the Arsenal players: talks which were addressed particularly to the new-comers, such as myself.

I arrived in London on a Sunday, and at once went into "digs" with a friend of the family from Exeter, who, like me, was an exile from Devon. The following day, I reported at Highbury.

I did not receive a very warm welcome. I was just walking through the main entrance, when I was stopped by the commissionaire.

"What do you want?" he asked. I felt a little surprised, and told him that I wanted to join the rest of the Arsenal players.

He patted me benevolently on the back, and began to edge me towards the door. "Well, sonny," he said, "you're a bit young at the moment. But never mind! One day you may be good enough to play for Arsenal!

It was only with the utmost difficulty that I managed to persuade him to fetch somebody outside to identify me. Eventually he brought out Joe Shaw, then the assistant manager, and looked painfully surprised when Joe vouched for me as a bone-fide Arsenal player!

I had just finished changing in the second team dressing-room, to which Joe conducted me, and had come out on to the road in training kit, ready to start the day in the Arsenal fashion, with some road work, when a little man with twinkling eyes came up to me, and introduced himself in an accent which I have never heard rivalled, before or since. It was Alex James. Little did I think, as we stood there talking together, that Alex and I were destined to form in the future one of the most discussed wings in the history of football.

I must confess that my chief reaction, apart from feeling rather more "at home" than I had done a few moments earlier, was one of intense concentration at trying to understand just what Alex was saying. Alex and I may have developed a well-nigh perfect understanding on the field, but off it, I have always found him a trifle incomprehensible!

Alex was, like me, a new-comer to Highbury. He had joined Arsenal from Preston North End shortly before I had been transferred from Exeter. The difference was that Alex was already the proud possessor of four Scottish international caps, while I came from an obscure team in the Third Division, of which I had not been a regular member for even three months!

Alex, of course, went into the first team at once. Since he cost Arsenal £9,000, it would have been somewhat surprising if he hadn't! I, on the other hand, was given a place in the reserves, as I fully expected. In those days, it was something of an honour, to be a regular member even of the Arsenal second string, and I was in no way disappointed that I did not make the first team right away.

It was as an inside-left that I played for the reserves. It had, of course, been my accustomed position for the past nine years. I found plenty of support in the Arsenal second team, and thoroughly enjoyed the matches I played for them. The Arsenal reserves had won the

Championship of the London Combination for the past three seasons, and we won it again in 1929-30, too.

Although, as I have said, I was perfectly content in the reserves, it was not long before I got my first chance in the first team. Arsenal started the season well enough, but a home defeat suffered at the hands of Bolton Wanderers, coming on top of a period of rather disappointing form, decided Mr. Chapman to make changes for the match the following Saturday, at Everton. David Jack was switched from inside-right to centre-forward, and I was brought in to take his place. The forward line as a whole read: Hulme, myself, Jack, Alex James and Charlie Jones. Charlie, of course, was our Welsh international "utility" man.

The match was a 1-1 draw, and this point was good enough to keep Arsenal in third place in the League table. Ritchie, deputising for Dixie Dean, as Everton's centre-forward, put his team ahead in the first half. Joe Hulme got our equaliser shortly after half-time.

I found it a thoroughly enjoyable game, and was particularly pleased to find that the pace was not too much for me. My only regret was that, after beating three Everton defenders, I shot straight at goalkeeper Davies, when only he was between me and the Everton net. I turned away rather disheartened, but Alex James was there with a consolatory pat on the back. "Never mind, Cliff," he said. "You did very well to get as far as you did."

"Watcher", of the *Daily Express*, had some kind words to say about me the following Monday. "When I consider," he wrote, "that Bastin was making his debut in First Division Football, there can be nothing but praise for this seventeen-year-old boy. He was fast, his judgement and shooting were sound, and he was easily the pick of the Arsenal line."

I stayed in for the next match, too. This was played against Derby County, at Highbury, and resulted in another 1-1 draw. I was fouled in the Derby penalty-box, eighteen minutes after the kick-off, and Tom Parker banged the ball home from the spot. Seven minutes later, he took another penalty – and missed it! Derby subsequently equalised our goal.

During the second half, I was switched to centre-forward. I had never played there before in my life, and I must confess I found things a little difficult. Certainly, I did not have as much success as I had enjoyed at Everton, although one writer praised me after the game for my "amazing coolness".

I was dropped for the match against Brentford in the London Cup, the following Wednesday – in those days, Arsenal used to field a full team in that competition – and went back into the reserve team for the next couple of months. My first team debut, by the way, took place on October 5th, 1929.

The player who impressed me most among my opponents, in my first two big matches, was undoubtedly Warney Cresswell, the Everton left-back, against whom I was destined to play many games in the future. I always found Warney a joy to play against. Unlike so many full-backs, he relied primarily on clever positioning, and bull-at-a-gate methods were entirely foreign to him. Admittedly, I found that his habit of backing away from the winger he was marking, when the latter received the ball, gave me time to take stock of the field and get the ball under control, but he was nevertheless a formidable opponent. He was, indeed the greatest back I ever played against.

It was not until Christmas Day that I was recalled to the first team. A few days before Christmas, Mr. Chapman called me up to his office, and informed me that I would be playing for the first team against Portsmouth, at outside-left. This was indeed a shock. It was quite a surprise to find that I was playing, but at outside left....Why, I hadn't played there since I was nine years old!

Mr. Chapman, however, possessed an almost hypnotic power of convincing. By the time I left his office, I felt as if I had been an established outside-left for years! As a matter of fact, Mr. Chapman's prime reason for putting me on the wing was for fear I might get knocked about as an inside-forward. He always had tremendous confidence in me – more, perhaps, than I had in myself – but I think he was almost as surprised as I was, when I achieved such prominence as an outside-left. Frankly, I still feel a little puzzled as to how I came to the top in this position. I have always regarded myself primarily as an inside-forward.

It is immensely difficult to convey to those who did not know Chapman an impression of his greatness – for I would not call it anything less than that. Perhaps I admired him more than others did, but I have always felt that the impressions of my Arsenal colleagues were the same as my own.

It was obvious that he had great confidence in himself, and he had the gift of transferring that confidence to others. I always felt that he knew football inside out. I never had any quarrels with him about the game, for I was invariably convinced that he was in the right. He was a very shrewd student of character, and would treat each person as an individual, possessed of his own peculiar strengths and weaknesses. If he said to me, as he sometimes did, "Go home for a week, Cliff, and forget all about football," I would go without question, knowing that it was the best thing for me. Pleasantly spoken, and rather on the short and stout side, there was nothing of the blustering bully about Chapman. Yet on a Monday morning at Highbury, when it was his habit to call up players to his office and talk about the previous Saturday's game, I always felt some trepidation lest I should be among those called up. Chapman, who gave few words of praise and fewer of blame, inspired awe and respect, rather than fear. He had complete command of us all.

When Christmas Day came round – and a nasty, sleety day it was, too – playing football was just about the last thing I felt like doing. London had not been agreeing with me, and I was in the midst of a series of violent bilious attacks. However, the club doctor passed me as fit, so there was nothing for it but to play.

I had quite a good game, in spite of my handicap, and we managed to beat Portsmouth – the game, by the way, was played at Fratton Park – by one goal to nil. Alex James was the scorer.

Somewhat against my will, I kept my place for the return match the next day, at Highbury. Incidentally, I had displaced Charlie Jones, who was naturally a little upset at losing his position. Charlie, who had come to us from Notts Forest, as an inside-forward, was not altogether Chapman's idea of an outside-left. In all fairness to Charlie, it must be remarked that he did not fancy himself in this position, either. "Good luck, Cliff," he had said to me, when he heard that I had taken his place. "I'm sick of outside-left, anyway." Charlie, of course, later turned into a wing-half, where he captained Arsenal and Wales in future seasons.

We lost the return game against Portsmouth, by the odd goal in three, thanks to a headed goal by the Portsmouth inside-left, Jimmy Easson, the ex-Scottish International who is now the Portsmouth trainer. Jimmy once had the curious experience of being chosen to play for England, whose selectors were unaware of his Scottish qualification! Subsequently, Scotland recognised his ability, so Jimmy got his cap after all!

I did fairly well in this Boxing Day game, making our only goal, which was scored by Joey Hulme, and hitting the post after a run through the Portsmouth defence. Illness did not seem to be affecting my play adversely.

The third match of the Christmas programme was away to Leeds United. I felt it exceptionally unlucky that I should be suffering from this stomach complaint just at the heaviest playing period of the season. And when I saw the conditions at Leeds I felt myself unluckier still.

Heavy rain was pelting down on the city, and the United pitch was a quagmire. If this wasn't bad enough, injuries forced Arsenal to field a skeleton team. Alf Baker, our right-half, had to play right-back, while David Jack took his place in the half-back line. Charlie Jones came back at inside-left, as substitute for Alex James. Consequently, it was no surprise when we lost by a couple of goals, both scored by the Leeds centre-forward, Jennings. Indeed the defeat might have been heavier still, had not our opponents obligingly missed a penalty.

Seldom have I been so glad to see the end of a game. Wet, cold and miserable, I shivered my way down the players' tunnel and into the dressing-room.

It was not until the close season that I managed to get rid of my bilious trouble. Curiously enough, I conquered the malady with cod-liver-oil tablets! They have never proved of any use to me before or since, yet they did enough in this particular instance to make me a cod-lover for ever more!

Apparently, I had done enough over Christmas to keep my place in the first team; still in my new and unaccustomed position; and I was included in the Arsenal line-up for our first match of the New Year, at home to Sheffield Wednesday.

So far as I was concerned, it was a successful game, but for the team as a whole it was not so happy. Alex James, back to the side once more, did not fit in, while David Jack, as leader of the attack, was obviously no solution to our centre-forward problem.

Consequently, we sustained out third successive defeat, this time going down by the odd goal in five. Little did we know it, however, but consolation was at hand!

4
THE ROAD TO WEMBLEY

I had found First Division football exciting enough, but it palled completely when the New Year came, bringing in its train the thrills and glamour which herald the Third Round of the F.A. Cup, when the First and Second Division clubs enter the arena.

I had gained my place in the Arsenal first team just in the nick of time, for barely a fortnight after the game against Portsmouth, at Fratton Park, we were scheduled to meet Chelsea, in a cup-tie at Highbury. I had yet to play in a Cup match, and found it a most alluring prospect.

Although the name of Arsenal had yet to be inscribed on the Cup, the general feeling at Highbury was that it was just about our turn. In the past four seasons we had been knocked out once in the Final, once in the Semi-Finals, and twice in the Sixth Round. So although on our only previous meeting with Chelsea they had defeated us 1-0 at Stamford Bridge, and gone on to lose in the Final – this was fifteen years previously – we felt reasonably confident that we would not go out at the first time of asking. Besides, Chelsea were a Second Division team, albeit a good one.

50,000 fans turned up to cheer at this local Derby, which we won fairly comfortably, 2-0. Jack Lambert, our centre-forward, played a storming game throughout, and scored our first goal. In the second half, a centre from Joey Hulme found me unmarked, and I scored my first ever goal for Arsenal. Incidentally, my selection on the left-wing came as rather a surprise in some quarters, where it had been expected that Charlie Jones would return.

A fortnight later we draw at Highbury 2-2 against Birmingham, in the Fourth Round. I scored our second goal, putting all I knew into a shot which whizzed past Harry Hibbs, struck the underside of the bar, and hit the back of the net.

We won the replay at Birmingham 1-0, thanks to a penalty goal by Alf Baker. The most notable feature of this game was that Alex James rose from his sick-bed to play in it, as substitute for Charlie Jones. Charlie never got back his place, for Alex at last proceeded to show the form which the football world expected of him.

An easy 2-0 victory at Middlesbrough; a 3-0 success at West Ham, and we were in the Semi-Final. Was this to be our year?

For the Semi-Final, we were drawn against Hull City, at the Leeds United ground. Hull were the shock team of the competition, for they had reached this late stage, in spite of the fact that they were in grave danger of relegation from the Second Division. As a matter of interest, they did get relegated at the end of the season.

However, they certainly didn't look like a relegation prospect in this Leeds Semi-Final. They quickly settled down, and shocked us by taking the lead in the fifteenth minute. And what a curious goal it was! Danny Lewis, our erratic Welsh International goal-keeping genius, ran out of his charge to scoop up a loose ball in the penalty area. So far, so good. Danny's clearance, however, travelled a mere thirty yards, and Howieson, the Hull inside-left, lobbed it back with the inside of his boot. This didn't perturb Danny unduly, and he calmly watched the ball pass over his head, for what he anticipated would be an innocuous goal-kick. Imagine his horror when the ball dipped suddenly in flight, and glided into the unguarded net!

Worse was to follow, for fourteen minutes later Eddie Hapgood sliced a shot from Duncan into his own goal. We were a very unhappy team at half-time. We all thought it wretched luck that we should present Hull with two gift goals within half an hour, when in the ordinary run of events two such mistakes wouldn't have occurred in half a season.

We were still two down after half the second period had elapsed. I was itching for the ball to run my way, for although I was not being "starved", the trend of the game had given me very little to do. At this stage of the game, Hull, who had come on top again, following some pressure by us, early in the half, suffered misfortune. Walsh, their right-half, was injured, and went on the wing; thus necessitating a team shuffle. Two minutes later we scored. Baker put Joey Hulme away on the right wing, and David Jack turned Joe's centre to good advantage.

The minutes ticked by. We were definitely in the ascendency now, but the vital goal just would not come. Hull City 2, Arsenal 1. Had yet another Arsenal team come so near but yet so far from a Wembley appearance, and victory? It seemed like it.

Suddenly came the chance for which I had been waiting. I had not even touched the ball for the last twenty minutes, and was longing to get into the thick of the battle. It was agony to stand idle on the wing, when we needed a goal so badly. Then, with eight minutes to go, Alex

James gave me the ball. Mills, the Hull deputy right-half, was there before me, but I managed to take the ball past him, into the middle, and crack it into the top right-hand corner of the net. There was little that Gibson, the Hull goalie, could do about it.

The relief of my Arsenal colleagues was remarkable to see. I was naturally very happy myself, but even in this moment my latent coolness did not desert me, with the result that I, who should have been the most excited of the whole team, was probably the least affected.

We drew the game 2-2, but came near to winning in the closing stages. After the final whistle, I was a trifle amused to find myself the hero of the moment. Amused because, apart from scoring that goal, I had barely touched the ball throughout the game. As it was, my team mates made a great fuss of me, while the wife of one of them overwhelmed me with enthusiastic attentions on the platform of the railway station.

Incidentally, the story of how we reached the station in time to catch our train provides a good example of what I, personally, considered one of Herbert Chapman's greatest qualities – his concern for the welfare of his players.

We were travelling to the station in a motor-coach – or, rather, we were trying to. Our coach was caught in the centre of an enormous traffic jam, and it looked as if we would be lucky to get to the station only an hour or so behind schedule. This wasn't good enough for Mr. Chapman. He stuck his head out of one of the windows of the coach, and roared protests at the policemen who were desperately trying to cope with the traffic confusion. He continued to do this at frequent intervals, much to the detriment of his imposing and hitherto impeccable black Homburg hat.

Eventually, Mr. Chapman's efforts brought their reward. Our coach was escorted through the traffic by a score of motor-cycle policemen: and we caught our train! A fine illustration not only of Mr. Chapman's care for our well-being, but of his formidable persuasive powers!

Our replay with Hull took place on the following Wednesday at Villa Park. It was not a particularly edifying game. We both seemed to retain memories of how we had shocked one another in turn, the previous Saturday. Consequently, neither side seemed to want to take the offensive, for fear of what might happen if it did. Not only that, but the Hull players seemed to be feeling some resentment for the way we had thwarted them the previous Saturday, and the result was a great deal of play which hardly befitted a Semi-Final. Indeed, the spectators might have been excused if they occasionally wondered whether certain Hull players were playing at La Savate, rather than football.

In the very different game which resulted, there is no doubt that the City had the better of the first half. Not very surprising, this, for it was difficult for us Arsenal forwards to combat successfully the rough methods of the Hull defence.

In point of fact, we only had one shot at the Hull goal throughout this period. That was when Joey Williams – back again instead of Joe Hulme – found himself with the ball at his feet, just fifteen yards away from the Hull goal: with only five minutes left to half-time. Unfortunately for us, he missed. So half-time came without any score.

Only five minutes of the second half had elapsed when Childs, the Hull centre-half, was sent off the field: and I never knew he had gone.

He had been playing what was, to say the least, rather a questionable game throughout, and had twice been cautioned by the referee. Eventually – as I discovered afterwards – he swung his foot at Jack Lambert, as the latter was going through for goal, and was promptly ordered off the field. It was done with such a lack of ostentation that the first intimation I had that something untoward had occurred was when I noticed that the City appeared to be somewhat depleted in numbers. For a while I couldn't make out whether this was merely my imagination, or whether the Gunners did now enjoy numerical superiority. At last I managed to pin down the discrepancy to the absence of the Hull City centre-half. I wondered what could have become of him.

"Where's Child's?" I asked Alex James.

"In the dressing-room," was the brief but pointed rejoinder.

Six minutes after this furtive departure we scored the only goal of the game. Most of the credit went to Joey Williams, who thereby atoned for his first-half miss.

Alex James began the movement, with one of his typical, swinging cross-field passes. As so often happened in such cases, the Hull defence was caught unawares. Joey Williams tore after the ball at terrific speed, pulled it back just as it was rolling over the touch-line; carried on down-wing like a veritable jet-plane, and finished by crossing the ball to David Jack's unerring right foot. David's volley was in the left-hand corner of the net before the unfortunate goalkeeper knew quite what was happening. That was the only goal of the game.

Every Arsenal player was heartily thankful when the final whistle was blown, giving us a respite from the violent tactics of the opposition. We knew it had been far from a great game, but felt – justifiably, I think – that the blame was not with us. Allied with this feeling of relief was one of supreme confidence. We all felt that if we could win the day against the methods we had been subjected to this afternoon, then there was little which could stop us winning the Final – never mind what had happened in 1927.

Earlier in this chapter, I recounted a little anecdote illustrative of the way in which Herbert Chapman always looked after his players. I can think of no better way of closing this chapter than to give another instance of the way Mr. Chapman looked after our welfare.

I was training one morning at Highbury, when a representative of a certain wrist-watch company arrived to see me. He informed me that his company wanted my permission to use my name, picture and recommendation on their advertisements. If I agreed, I would be rewarded with one of their watches for my services.

"Just a minute," I said, "I must speak to Mr. Chapman about this."

Needless to say, we players always sought his advice in all such matters. Accordingly, I went to him in his office, and asked him what reply I should make to the representative of the watch company, who was waiting below.

"Send him up here!" said Chapman.

When I had brought the man into his office Mr. Chapman lowered at him for a moment or two, then said: "I understand you are from the —— Watch Company?"

"Why, yes," said the man, looking a trifle uncomfortable, "I am."

"And you have offered one of my players a three-guinea watch for the use of his name on your advertisements?"

"Yes, I have."

Then Chapman really exploded. "Here is this young man, right at the top of his profession, and you mean to tell me you dare to offer him a miserable three-guinea watch?"

"Well," mumbled the unhappy object of this tirade, "it isn't my fault. I was told to. Anyway, we offered So-and-so (naming a famous jockey) the same, and he accepted."

Mr. Chapman looked at him with a mixture of wrath and pain. "You don't mean to say," he asked, "that you put Arsenal in the same class as a wretched jockey?"

After a few minutes more of this treatment the watch-firm representative made for the door, and the negotiations – if one can call them such – were abruptly broken off. He had not been authorised to offer any greater remuneration.

When the door closed behind him I turned to Mr. Chapman.

"Thanks very much for looking after me like this, Mr. Chapman," I said, "but I can't help feeling sorry for that poor fellow who has just gone out."

Mr. Chapman looked up with a twinkle in his eye. "Well, Cliff," he said, "between ourselves, if it had been me, I would have taken the watch right away! But for you, I wanted to get something better!"

5
WE WIN THE F.A. CUP

Our opponents in the Cup Final were to be Huddersfield Town. The Town had eliminated their fellow-Yorkshiremen, Sheffield Wednesday, by two goals to one, in the Semi-Final played at Old Trafford.

Nobody could reasonably have asked for a more attractive and intriguing last pair. True, Huddersfield had been giants for the past ten years, whereas Arsenal were only in the early stages of their successes. This, however, was beside the point. What really mattered was that Herbert Chapman had brought Huddersfield to the top and now, barely four years later, he was the man behind the successes of Arsenal.

Nor was this all. The match was one of those glamorous North *versus* South affairs, which arouse the interest of not only the supporters of the teams in question, but of other clubs, all over the country. No London side had won the Cup since the Spurs did the trick nine years earlier. This, with the other Tottenham success in 1901, was the only time the coveted trophy had come to London.

There was no doubt that Huddersfield were going to provide us with powerful opposition. Admittedly, all their successes but one had been by the odd goal, and that – against Bury – was a replay, but they had only once been held to a draw, while it will be remembered that we had twice to try again.

Their team included no less than seven internationals, to our six, of who Jackson and Kelly, the right-wing pair, had gained very nearly thirty caps between them. It was from Alex Jackson that we feared most. This dashing, happy-go-lucky Scot, who possessed an uncomfortable knack of popping up in the goal mouth, just when he was least expected, had been the hero of Scotland's 1928 win against England at Wembley. Then, he had scored three times in their astonishing 5-1 victory. He had been personally responsible for no less than nine of Huddersfield's eleven Cup goals.

As against this, we possessed another star of the "Wee Blue Devil" forward-line, which had made England look so foolish two years ago. This was Alex James. By the time the Final came around, Alex had almost recaptured the form he had shown that day. He had come to Highbury from Preston with a reputation made as a goal scorer, rather than a schemer, and it took some time before Chapman's ambition to convert him from the one category into the other proved successful.

Alex Jackson apart, everyone else at Highbury was pretty confident of success. Mr. Chapman, somewhat naturally, knew the Huddersfield team and tactics absolutely inside out, and he made full use of his knowledge. After he had expounded the strengths and weaknesses of our opponents to our entire satisfaction, he concentrated on the problem which was worrying us all – how we were going to stop Alex Jackson. By the time he had finished, we felt reasonably sure that, provided none of our defenders had an off-day, we would probably be able to do that, too.

A week before the great game was due, the Arsenal team and reserves travelled down to Brighton, to partake once more the delights of South Coast air. This had been a regular ritual, before every cup-tie we had played this year.

We all awaited the Final with mingled feelings of excitement and apprehension. Those of us who had played in the Arsenal side which had so unluckily lost to Cardiff, in the 1927 Cup Final, had fears that the bad fortune which had dogged us that day might again spoil our chances, in the game against Huddersfield. However, to console us, there was the fact that we had trounced the Town 2-0 in the League, at Highbury, while holding them to a 2-2 draw on their own ground.

We were so busy enjoying ourselves down at Brighton, however, that there wasn't much time for reflection, morbid or otherwise. Much of our time was taken up by golf, and we were frequent visitors to the local Dyke Golf Club. Of course, we had to keep in training on the football field, too, and for this purpose we used the Brighton and Hove Albion ground.

With a couple of humorists like Joey Hulme and Alex James in the party there was bound to be plenty of fun, and the incident which I am about to recount will serve to show how high the morale was amongst us.

The scene was the bar of the Dyke Golf Club, where a number of us were taking liquid refreshment – in moderation, of course! There was a telephone on the bar itself, and suddenly it began to jangle. It was a call for our goalkeeper, Charlie Preedy.

Charlie put the receiver to his ear, and was informed by the caller at the other end that he was a sporting journalist, who wanted a story on the Cup Final for his paper. Would Charlie be so kind as to give him one?

Now, all this may seem fairly straightforward – as it did to Charlie himself – but the fact was that the "journalist" at the other end was none other than Joey Hulme, phoning from the secretary's office, next door. All of us were in on the secret except Charlie, who was completely deceived by Joe's cunningly disguised voice.

Charlie was interested in what he took to be a perfectly serious proposition. He said that he would gladly grant his interviewer a few words on the forthcoming Final, but first he would have to ask Mr. Chapman's permission. Joe said that he hoped Mr. Chapman would grant this permission, and that if he did there would be £50 waiting for Charlie. On receipt of this information Charlie's face brightened perceptibly, and we all guessed that Joe had mentioned money! It was with the utmost difficulty that we prevented ourselves from giving way to gusts of laughter, but we all managed to keep our faces straight, although there were a few suppressed chuckles when Charlie left the bar-room to seek Mr. Chapman's assent.

Our manager was in the secret, too, and this assent was readily granted. The delighted Charlie scampered back to the telephone, and informed a very interested Joe Hulme that he did not feel in the least nervous, was very hopeful of an Arsenal win, and looked forward to appearing at Wembley.

Joey listened for a few minutes, then, tiring of his impersonation, relapsed into his usual broad Yorkshire dialect, and suggested to an astonished Charlie that he should join him in a drink, at the bar. Charlie, of course, recognised his voice at once. I fear that his reply was quite unprintable!

At last Saturday, April 26th, came round, and we climbed into a motor coach at Harrow, where we had lunched, off on the road to Wembley. Alex James seemed the least affected by the forthcoming ordeal. He chattered merrily away in his unintelligible accent for most of the drive. When our journey was half completed, he turned to me and said: "If we get a free-kick, Cliff, and it's in my section of the field, I'm going to slip you a quick pass. I want you to draw the defence, then let me have the ball back, and I'll crash it into the net!"

There was loud laughter from all and sundry at Alex's "prophecy", for his reputation as a marksman had been left behind at Preston, and he had not scored a single goal throughout our Cup run.

Yet, in point of fact, his was no mere idle boast, as we were destined to see.

In our dressing-room, Bert Rutt, our groundsman, played record after record to us on his gramophone, in an endeavour to take our minds off the match which was soon to follow. Meanwhile, the roar of over 90,000 voices uplifted in community singing vied with Bert's gramophone recital for first place in our attentions.

There was no doubt who was the most nervous of our number – Tom Parker, our right back and captain; though by all rights, I suppose it ought to have been me. It was only a little over a month ago that I had passed my eighteenth birthday – a fact which made me the youngest player ever to appear in a Cup Final. Tom, however, obviously retained memories of the Final three years ago. Then, as everybody knows, Arsenal, under Tom's captaincy, had seemed to have the beating of Cardiff City. Then came tragedy. A long shot by Cardiff centre-forward Ferguson; a save by Danny Lewis; a fumble; another fumble; and the ball was in our net. Tom was obviously turning over and over in his mind the prospects of Charlie Preedy – never the most reliable of goalkeepers – repeating Lewis' blunder today.

As for me, I was feeling fairly comfortable in my mind, in spite of the fact that I would be facing Roy Goodall, then the regular England right-back, and one of the most formidable defenders in the four countries. My only trouble was that I appeared to have swallowed a butterfly, *en route* to the Stadium, and the insect persisted in fluttering about in the pit of my stomach!

At length, the time came for the teams to take the field, and we walked out of the tunnel into the warm sunshine, relishing the feel of the green, springy turf. We came out side by side with Huddersfield. It was the first time this had ever been done in a Cup Final, and was the outcome of a suggestion made by Herbert Chapman. Since then it has always been the custom.

It must have been a proud moment for Mr. Chapman, when the two clubs which he had made great took the field shoulder to shoulder, on this already momentous occasion.

We stood to attention whilst the National Anthem was played by the band of the Welsh Guards; then the teams were introduced to His Majesty King George V. As we were standing to attention, while His Majesty shook hands with each player in turn, my gaze turned towards the crowd. My mother and father were sitting amongst those thousands of people. I knew roughly where they were, and suddenly I spotted them, and waved a greeting, which they returned. It may have been rather an incongruous thing to do, at that particular moment, but whether it was or not, this little incident gave me terrific confidence. It was grand to know that, no matter what the great mass of spectators was shouting, there were two people amongst them whose thoughts and hopes were centred on me. The butterfly in my stomach ceased its fluttering; I felt a thrill of pleasurable anticipation run through me; and I felt capable of facing any back in the world – including Roy Goodall.

The inspection over, both teams had the usual short kicking-in at goal, then the players went to their places. This was how the teams lined up:

Arsenal: Preedy; Parker (captain); Hapgood; Baker; Seddon; John; Hulme; Jack; Lambert; James; myself.

Huddersfield Town: Turner; Goodall; Spence; Naylor; Wilson; Campbell; Jackson; Kelly; Davies; Raw; Smith.

It was a terrific, end-to-end battle from the start. The ultimate score might point to a comparatively easy victory for us, but this was very far from the case. The blue-and-white stripes of Huddersfield were swarming around our goal mouth, time and time again, but we were giving them a good as we received.

As I had mentioned, it was Alex Jackson who caused us the most trouble. Outside-left Billy Smith, who scored over two hundred goals in League Football, was a problem, too; but we didn't mind him so much. Billy was content to whizz up and down the touch-line, whereas Jackson, as usual, was popping up here, there and everywhere.

Fortunately for us, Eddie Hapgood was in brilliant form. He had strict instructions to follow Jackson around like Mary's little lamb, and he carried them out to the letter. Apart from myself, Eddie was the youngest player on the field. He had only recently celebrated his twenty-first birthday.

Our two reserve players were putting up vividly contrasting displays. Bill Seddon, the substitute at centre-half for the still injured Herbie Roberts, was doing all that was asked of him. He was making good use of the one-inch superiority in height he enjoyed over Davies, the Huddersfield centre-forward, with the consequence that high balls down the middle did not cause any qualms in the Arsenal camp.

Charlie Preedy, who had taken the place of Danny Lewis – also injured – was playing a very different type of game to the solid, if somewhat uninspired, Bill.

The programme pen-picture of Charlie had said of him: "Preedy never hesitates to leave his goal if he thinks the occasion demands such a measure. After all, it's odds on the goalkeeper who advances at the right time. Better than "stopping at home" and having to pick the ball out of the net, says Charlie."

Now, I am all in favour of the goalkeeper who, as the Programme put it, "advances at the right time". On this particular occasion, however, Charlie was advancing all the time - whether it was the right time or the wrong time was purely incidental! On almost every appearance of the ball in the Arsenal penalty area, Charlie, to quote the Programme again, thought "the occasion demanded such a measure". True, he may have liked it better than "stopping at home" and "having to pick the ball out of the net", but when one really gets down to brass tacks, the difference between this and diving among the legs of opposing attackers, only to achieve the same result, is not very important!

Indeed, I would have said that the first alternative would have been the better of the two. The goalkeeper who is beaten whilst standing on his goal-line doesn't have to go back so far to pick the ball out of his net!

Be that as it may, Charlie's far too daring antics nearly caused heart failure among his colleagues, and I am sure that, had Tom Parker not been practically bald, his hair would have been turned grey! For there was Charlie, rushing out of his goal at every other moment; either missing the ball completely, or making a brilliant save! To call his display erratic would be a miserable understatement!

I was finding Roy Goodall a formidable opponent, as I had expected, but I was giving him just about as good as I got, and was causing him a considerable amount of trouble. It must have been really intriguing to the vast crowd, this duel between the veteran captain of England and an eighteen-year-old boy.

With the game seventeen minutes old, neither side had scored, although we had both come very near to doing so. Then.... it happened! Alex James was fouled, half-way inside the Huddersfield half. He swooped on the ball, placed it on the correct spot, and with a yell of "Back, Cliff!" booted it out to me. In a flash, his words in the coach came back to me: "I want you to draw the defence, then let me have the ball back." I took the ball up the wing, drawing Roy Goodall slowly but surely out of the centre. Out of the corner of my eye I could see that, in the penalty area, the attention of the Huddersfield defenders was focused almost entirely on Lambert and David Jack. It was just what I wanted. At the last possible moment, I slipped the ball inside to Alex James, and he, true to his word, took it on a few paces, then slammed it past Turner and into the back of the net. We were one up!

That goal made us a good deal more confident. The first goal in a big match is always vitally important, and no team scoring it in a Wembley Cup Final had yet failed to emerge as victors. With a little more steadiness, we might have been three up by half-time, for Joey Hulme and Jack Lambert both fell victims to nerves, and thus missed a couple of good scoring opportunities. However, it would have been thoroughly unjust if we had obtained these two goals, for we were lucky to be one goal ahead, let alone three.

As we relaxed in the dressing-room at half-time we were a happy but somewhat apprehensive team. Happy, because we were a goal in the lead; apprehensive, because we knew that the game was far from being won, and that the Town's forwards were perfectly capable of summarily ending our rejoicing.

Fortunately, our defence kept up their grand work throughout the second half. The backs and half-backs were solidity itself, and although the same could not have been said of Charlie Preedy, his inconsistency did not bring any disaster in its wake. Eddie Hapgood had really got the measure of Alex Jackson, while his task was made considerably easier by the iron grip which Bob John kept on his namesake, Bob Kelly, Jackson's inside forward. Bill Seddon was thoroughly enjoying himself, and centre-forward Davies could not make anything of his terrific tackling.

Nevertheless, it was not until seven minutes from time that we Arsenal players really felt at ease. It was Jack Lambert who set our doubts at rest. Alex James belted the a long pass down the centre of the field – the type of pass which he excelled in making, and which had been causing agonies in the Huddersfield camp on numerous occasions.

Jack gathered the ball, shook off a tackle from Wilson, and dashed through unopposed to score our second goal. It was a fitting reward to a great-hearted player.

That was the end of Huddersfield. They could not reasonably hope to score two goals against our grand defence, in the few minutes that remained. When the final whistle blew, the Cup had come to Highbury for the first time ever. I shall always remember the roar which came from the throats of the thousands of Arsenal supporters present when the referee Tom Crew signalled the end of the game.

It was a proud moment for me when I received my winners' medal from King George V, and I was doubly happy by the knowledge that my mother and father were there to see it happen.

I had left Exeter City less than a year ago, and I had never even visualised playing in a Cup-winning side at all when I signed – let alone within such a short space of time. Still, there it was. I was barely eighteen years old, and I had not only been a member of the victorious side, but had made the all-important first goal.

Little did I guess that two more Cup Final medals – one of them a winners' – five League Championship medals, and twenty-one international caps were to follow.

With Exeter City – The start of Bastin's career.

Cliff Bastin aged seventeen.

The English Team; Schools' International Match, Aberdare, 1926

Arsenal team for the F.A. Cup Final, 1931-32

Herbert Chapman

Cliff Bastin taking a corner at Highbury.

England team *versus* Italy, 1933

Italy *versus* England match, Rome, 1933.

6
OUR RECORD SEASON

Season 1930 saw Arsenal's first ever triumph in the F.A. Cup Final; in fact, the first ever triumph in a competition of major importance. It was the beginning of the era in which Arsenal dominated the football world. Herbert Chapman had impregnated the players around him with the confidence and fighting spirit with which he himself was imbued, and the results were destined to be amazing.

Arsenal – and I myself – started off the 1930-31 campaign on the right foot. The first Arsenal trial, played a few weeks before the League Championship started, was described by one newspaper correspondent as "one of the best ever seen at Highbury". The team which had defeated Huddersfield in the Cup Final – which, of course, included myself – met a side containing players of the calibre of Joey Williams, Charlie Jones, and David Halliday. After an exciting struggle, the Cup team won 5-3, and I had the pleasure of scoring three of the goals.

The man who kept goal for the losing side was a newcomer to Highbury: Gerry Keizer. Gerry was a Dutchman. A wholesale fruiterer by vocation, he never forsook his amateur status, even when he joined Charlton Athletic, in later years. Gerry, mildly crazy, and utterly fearless, whether on the field or off it – characteristics he shared with almost every good goalkeeper who has ever played in the English League – was a very good friend of mine.

When I say that he was mildly crazy, I do not want this to be taken too literally. I merely want to signify that Gerry was utterly and incredibly reckless, whether between the posts of the Arsenal goal, or crouched behind the wheel of one of the huge American cars which were his heart's delight.

Like most Continental footballers of my acquaintance, Gerry was very excitable and, as such, was inconsistent. His style, after the fashion of all European goalkeepers, was spectacular. He was master of his own penalty area, never having the slightest hesitation in coming out to gather a high ball. He could play games equal to the best one could imagine, and had he taken the game a little more seriously he might have attained great heights.

Our first match of the new season, in which we fielded our Cup-winning team, with the exception of Charlie Jones for Alf Baker at right half, was away to the newly promoted Blackpool. We could hardly have made a better start. I scored from a penalty in the first half, and we were consequently a goal in the lead at half-time. Yet the Arsenal dressing-room, during the interval, certainly did not resemble a mutual admiration society. On the contrary, it was a buzz of earnest voices. "You should have done this," "We ought to do that," "They might do so-and-so," was the portent of the many different voices raised in self-analysis. Once again, it was the Chapman spirit taking effect. He had taught us never to lean back on our laurels, however well-earned they might be.

Our eagerness for improvement bore fruit in the second half, when we rammed home three more goals. I scored the second, it was a goal which will always stick in my memory. I closed in to a centre from Joey Hulme, and volleyed it as hard as I knew how to with my right foot. The ball whizzed past the Blackpool goalkeeper, struck one of the iron supports inside the goal, and came bouncing out again. It all happened so quickly that I suspect few people in the crowd knew quite what was happening. Certainly, the goalkeeper didn't.

Little time was afforded to us to pat ourselves on the back, after this success, for on the following Monday, a bare two days later, we faced Bolton Wanderers, in an away game at Burnden Park. The result? Another 4-1 win. We just did not seem able to put a foot wrong. Gerry Keizer made his Arsenal debut in that game, but the most noteworthy achievement was a brilliant hat-trick by Jack Lambert, our lion-hearted centre-forward.

Three goals in a League game is always an excellent performance, but on this occasion it was even more meritorious, for the man between the Bolton posts that day was classic Dick Pym.

Devon-born like myself, Dick, one of football's gentlemen, had been a schoolboy idol of mine. His clean handling, wonderful anticipation and long kicking made him one of the finest goalkeepers of his day. He played three times in the Cup Final at Wembley – and never gave away a goal. Only his ingrained sensitiveness prevented him from becoming the greatest goalkeeper of all time.

One other Devonshire man I used to meet on visits to Bolton was Harold Blackmore, their centre-forward. Before I joined Exeter City, I used to watch Harold leading their attack. His powerful display in a benefit game between Exeter and Bolton led to his transfer to the Lancashire team, with whom he won a Cup Final medal. Harold was the possessor of a left foot whose strength was second to none, and, although not a great player, I thought that he might at least have gained one England cap.

The Saturday after our defeat of Bolton we had our first game of the season at Highbury, against Leeds United, which did not call for any special mention. We won fairly easily, 3-1. Then Blackburn Rovers came to town, and very nearly held us to a draw, thanks to the brilliance of their fine inside-right, Syd Puddefoot. I had a successful game, scoring in the very first minute, and getting the last of our three goals, too. 3-2 was the score.

The next few weeks saw the Arsenal steam-roller flatten one team after another. Following our eight goals in our two first away games, we scored four each in our next two as well, and recorded our best ever start to a season, by winning the first six matches.

As one victory succeeded another, so the opposition became more and more tough. Indeed, in that season, and the ones which were to follow, it was always a terrific strain playing for Arsenal. Every club went flat out to beat us. All of them pulled out just that little bit extra, in an endeavour to lower the colours of Chapman's "Wonder Team".

Our winning run came to an end when Sheffield United held us to a 1-1 draw, at Highbury. Jimmy Dunne, their Goliath-like, fair-headed centre-forward, was the man who scored their goal. Jimmy was in terrific form at that period, and netted hat-tricks in each of the two preceding Sheffield games. Later, of course, he came to Arsenal, but by then he was past his best. At the height of his career, I ranked Jimmy one of the five best centre-forwards I have ever seen. Herbert Chapman tried to bring him to Highbury for a long, long time. It was ironic that, when at last he did so, it was too late.

Derby County eventually put an end – temporarily only, however – to our run of success. The week after our draw with Sheffield, we met them at the Baseball Ground, three days after defeating Sheffield Wednesday in the F.A. Charity Shield. Derby got down to business while we were still warming up, and before thirty minutes had gone by they were three goals in the lead. We settled down, then. I sent in a cross-drive, which hit the back of the Derby net, and centre-half Herbie Roberts came up to score a second. But just as we seemed likely to gain a great triumph over our depressing start, and over injuries to several of our players, George Stephenson popped up, to net a fourth for Derby. A rumbling cheer went round the football world. Arsenal had at last been beaten.

In a way, we were glad to lose our unbeaten record, although we felt that we had been rather unlucky in doing so. Now, we thought, the other clubs would not pull that little bit more out of the bag, in an endeavour to be the first to lower our colours. We were wrong. In the future, of course, almost every opponent played on the top of its form, whether we were enjoying an unbeaten run or not. As I have already said, this made it a strain to play for Arsenal – but it also kept one very much on one's toes.

As a result of this defeat, Aston Villa, with centre-forward Pongo Waring in brilliant form, jumped above us to the top of the League, on goal average. But we pulled ourselves together again, and when the day came for Villa's visit to Highbury we were a couple of points ahead. Everybody expected this to be a close and classic game, but we surprised most people by giving the Villa a 5-2 beating. 64,000 roared their heads off at the game, but although Pongo Waring scored two goals, two from David Jack, another from Jack Lambert, and a couple from myself gave us a comfortable victory. "I never hope to see a better match," said L. V. Manning of the *Daily Sketch*.

Yet we could not manage to draw clear of our pursuers, at the top of the table. Sheffield Wednesday, with the great Strange, Leach, Wilson half-back line, took over the baton from Villa, and overhauled us on goal average, although we had a game in hand. "Lucky Arsenal" they were calling us, mainly for the way Eddie Hapgood and Tom Parker – especially Eddie – scraped ball after ball off the Arsenal goal-line. But we didn't care – we just did our best to keep on winning.

I began to believe in bogeys when Newcastle United smashed our unbeaten home record, the week before Christmas. The reason was that Bedford, their inside-right, was the main cause of our defeat, scoring a goal. A few months previously, he had done more or less the same thing, playing for Derby County.

We had a very happy Christmas, however, winning all our games, and the New Year saw us happily ensconced at the top of the League – the proud possessors of a four-point lead. An interesting feature of our Christmas programme was that George Male made his Arsenal debut, as left-half, in the match against Blackpool, which we won, incidentally 7-1. "An exceedingly promising display," beamed one sports writer, referring to George.

Our goalkeeper about this time was Bill Harper. Bill, of course, had played for Arsenal and Scotland in previous years, but he had gone to America for a period, and only kept goal for Arsenal at this stage of my career with them. Bill, rather past his best by then, had acquired a number of American mannerisms and habits. He had developed the usual Transatlantic breezy bonhomie, and impaired his training considerably by smoking innumerable pungent cigars. But he still had much of his old skill, and I was impressed by his powerful kicking.

With the turn of the year came, of course, the prospect of the F.A. Cup, of which we were the holders. No matter what our position was in the Championship, we always had a try at winning the Cup, and especially was this so when we were heading the League. Then hopes of the double rose into view.

We were drawn against Villa in the first – or Third – round. Confident of beating them, as we had already done once that season, they shocked us by scoring an early goal. The ground was a slippery morass, and Bill Harper perhaps was not altogether to be blamed for letting an easy-looking shot skid through his hands into the net. Billy Walker headed number two from a corner, and it looked as if the Cup Winners were out.

But Villa were lucky to be ahead, and steady pressure by us brought its reward when Alex James, who was appearing here, there and everywhere, made a goal for Jack Lambert. Even Herbie Roberts nearly scored in our subsequent heavy pressure, but it was not until a few minutes from time that David Jack put us out of our misery when he crashed his way into the Villa net, taking the ball and goalkeeper with him. We won the replay 3-1 on another appalling day.

Next stop – and last, did we but know it – Stamford Bridge. That, of course, meant Chelsea. We had knocked them out of the Cup last year, smashed them 5-1 in the League a little while back, and, not knowing our Chelsea, expected to do the trick once more on this occasion.

It was a day of gusty wind, and an unsafe Bill Harper. Chelsea scored after a corner, and young George Mills put them farther ahead, with a grand header from Alex Jackson's cross. We had been playing a poor game, well below our normal standard, and by the time we woke up it was too late. Our only goal came when a David Jack – Jack Lambert move found me unmarked, and I raced Millington to the ball, to put it into the net. Just on time, we thought we had the equaliser, when Millington was caught yards out of position, for a stinging shot. But

Barber, the Chelsea right-back, headed out from underneath the bar, and that was that.

Andy Ducat, the famous old Arsenal and Aston Villa right-half, summed matters up, when he wrote in the *Sunday Dispatch*: "It was difficult to recognise Arsenal, who had one of those bad days that come to every team." He had a few kind words for me, however: "Only Bastin, the youngest of the five, showed coolness and decision in the Arsenal attack. He scored a good goal, and kept his head when others were flustered."

A blessing in disguise? Perhaps it was, for, left to concentrate on the League, we went on to set up a points record which had not been approached to this day.

The Wednesday after our defeat at Stamford Bridge we compensated ourselves to a great extent by walloping Grimsby Town, 9-1. This game had been postponed some weeks back. Fog had led to its abandonment. I was rather surprised at the weak resistance Grimsby put up, for in the abandoned game they had been playing very well, and were only a single goal behind, when proceedings were adjourned. I had to be content with one goal out of the nine; David Jack and Jack Lambert were responsible for most of the others.

We took joyous revenge on Derby County, a few weeks later, cracking home six goals to their three. I had a good day, getting half our total.

So, still hounded by Sheffield Wednesday and the Villa, we remained at the head of the First Division, unable to relax for a moment, even had we wanted to do so. I do not want to bore my readers with endless match description. Besides, I must confess that it is but few games that stick in my memory. Personalities, rather than incidents, have left their impression on me.

Take, for instance, a Saturday afternoon in March; the scene – Villa Park, crammed full with seventy thousand spectators. An injury to Alex James upset the Arsenal rhythm, and we crashed to a 5-1 defeat. The memory of the game is not particularly clear in my mind – after a lapse of nearly two decades, perhaps this is not surprising – but when I think of it, I think of a personality which stands out very clearly indeed – Aston Villa's Pongo Waring.

Pongo was an amazing character. Whenever Arsenal were playing Villa, and Pongo was in his usual role of centre-forward in the Villa team, he would make a point of button-holing the illustrious

Herbert Chapman. "You'd like to buy me, wouldn't you, Herbert?" he would chuckle. Chapman, aghast, would offer no reply.

One man who never liked playing against Pongo was our goalkeeper, Charlie Preedy. Pongo, a very big fellow, would breathe mock threats at him. "I'm going to get you this time, Charlie," he would glower. In jest as such menaces undoubtedly were, Charlie implicitly believed every word of them. His play always suffered as a result. On the occasion of this 5-1 affair, he leapt frantically here, there and everywhere – but mostly somewhere that the ball was not. The burly Pongo seemed always just beside him – however far away he really might be. Shortly before this game, by the way, I had played at Highbury for England v The Rest – my first international trial.

Our Villa Park defeat made little difference to us. We moved steadily on towards the Championship, and after a 1-0 win at Grimsby the newspapers told us that we had broken the record for points scored away from home; needed but one more to set up a new points record altogether; and with two more would gain our first Championship. We were mildly interested, but not particularly excited. At Highbury, Chapman taught us to take things in our stride. One success must be the prelude to another. There was no time for empty self-congratulation.

We won the League all right, the following Saturday, although we made a rather nervous start against Liverpool. Herbie Roberts putting through his own goal after a bare three minutes. But we settled down to our normal game; Jack Lambert equalised, I put us ahead, and then swung over a corner, for David Jack to make things certain. The Championship was ours. We went on to win our last two games as well, thereby beating the existing Championship record by fully half a dozen points.

This Arsenal team of 1930-31 was the finest eleven I ever played in. And, without hesitation, I include in that generalisation international teams as well. Never before had there been such a team put out by any club – and never since have I seen it rivalled.

7
MY FIRST INTERNATIONAL

On a grey, November day in 1931 a certain young man bought an evening newspaper, looked anxiously at the sports page, and leapt an appreciable height into the air. The young man was none other than myself. I had just learned that I had been picked for England.

I am jumping a little ahead of my subject, however, I have already mentioned that I took part in an international trial towards the end of the 1930-31 season. That took place, of course, in March. It did not bring any results so far as I was concerned, for Crawford, of Chelsea, was chosen as outside-left against Scotland, the following April.

Nor did I come into the picture – not that I expected to – for the first representative game in which I was eligible to play the following season – that between the Football League and the Irish League. Eric Houghton of Aston Villa was the selected outside-left. Little did I know it, though, but a great thrill was in store for me. When the team was announced to represent the Football League against the Scottish League, in Glasgow, I was included!

It was a surprise selection, not only to myself, but to the football public as well. Eric Houghton had been strongly tipped to keep his place in the side, for he had followed a convincing display against the Irish League with a good showing on the English wing against Ireland herself, on the occasion of England's 6-2 win in Belfast.

The Football League team was: Hibbs (Birmingham); Goodall (Huddersfield); Blenkinsopp (Sheffield Wednesday); Edwards (Leeds United); Graham (Nottingham Forest); Edwards, J. (West Bromwich); Crooks (Derby County); Smith (Portsmouth); Dean (Everton); Bestall (Grimsby Town); myself.

The Scottish League side, which included but few of the Scottish team recently defeated by Ireland, looked certain to provide worthy opposition for our powerful team. Among the famous names which were to face us were David Meiklejohn, the great Rangers right-half-back, Jimmy McGrory, destined to become the most prolific goal scorer in the history of football, and the legendary Alan Morton. From him I hoped to learn much, although this great outside-left was in the last stages of his magnificent career.

Accordingly, I trotted on to the field at Celtic Park on the afternoon of Wednesday, November 7th, my head high up among the clouds, and the kindly good wishes of my Arsenal colleagues ringing in my ears. At nineteen years old, I was easily the youngest player in the match. A huge crowd had assembled in the hope of watching the Scottish League take some measure of revenge for the crushing 7-3 defeat which the Football League had inflicted on them at Tottenham, the previous year.

This, then, was the setting for my first representative game. And what a game it was! After only seven minutes, Sammy Crooks put through an accurate pass to Jack Smith, our inside-right, for the latter to put us ahead. Then the Scots took over. Big Jimmy McGrory wiped out our lead, after we had enjoyed it for only three minutes, and to remind us further that we were playing on the Glasgow Celtic ground, Jimmy's club colleague, Celtic left-back McGonagle, beat Harry Hibbs from the penalty spot.

A third from the great Bob McPhail meant that we had our backs to the wall, facing a 3-1 deficit.

I was enjoying the game a good deal, myself. Although the Scots had so far had more of the play, I had nevertheless been given plenty to do, and had fared quite well in my tussles with Crapnell, the Scottish right-back.

A bare second before half-time, I experienced the great thrill of scoring a goal in my first representative game. Dixie Dean, Everton's hefty centre-forward, got the ball, and started dribbling towards the left-wing. I instinctively moved inside to take his place in the centre. It proved a successful manoeuvre. Just at the right moment, Dixie swung the ball across the Scottish goal, and I banged it in past Johnny Jackson, into the back of the net. If you'd wanted to find the happiest man in Scotland, you wouldn't have had to look any farther than where I was standing!

This was the first of many games I was destined to play against Johnny Jackson. He, like me, was making his debut in representative games, that day. Then attached to Partick Thistle, he later, of course, moved south of the Border to Chelsea.

I had an exhilarating second half. I enjoyed every minute of it, and I suppose I have seldom played better. I scored again, to wipe out Scotland's lead, and it looked as if we might even turn what had once seemed a certain defeat into a grand victory. Unfortunately, Jimmy

McGrory had other ideas on the subject. A chance came his way in the closing stages of the game, and Harry Hibbs's gallant effort to save was all in vain.

I was disappointed that we had lost, but felt supremely happy that I had enjoyed such a successful game, on my representative debut. Much of this success was undoubtedly due to the shrewd prompting of my partner at inside-left, Jackie Bestall.

Jackie was the captain of Grimsby Town for many years. So great was the service he rendered to the club that a street was named after him, on his retirement. Now manager of Blackburn Rovers, Jackie certainly helped me that day.

The newspaper critics were very kind to me after this game, and in the ensuing week I was strongly tipped for inclusion in the England team to meet Wales at Anfield Road, Liverpool, on November 18th - eleven days after the League international.

Consequently, when, as I have already recounted at the beginning of the chapter, I saw in an evening newspaper that I had been picked for the game, my pleasure at this honour was rather greater than my surprise. Modesty apart, there can't be much surprise in your selection, when the National Press has been prophesying it at you for the past seven days!

I often used to wish that I had never become an outside-left, when the time came round for international teams to be announced. It was just agony to be forced to wait, while a radio announcer read slowly through the list of eleven names, until at long, long last he came to mine! Of course, it was a different matter when my first intimation of the team for which I hoped to be chosen came from a newspaper. Then my eyes went straight to the end of the list!

It was different, too, when I was picked in one of the inside-forward positions, as did occasionally happen. Mostly, however, I was chosen on the wing.

Some of my readers may not realise that it is seldom, if ever, from the Football Association that a player received the news that he has been picked for an international. The first communication he gets from them is the itinerary, which arrives a day or two after the team has been announced.

The Press and radio, of course, are informed of the composition of international teams as soon as these are selected, and thus become the mediums whereby the players themselves are informed. I remember one particular occasion when I learned that I had been picked for England against Scotland while driving in my car, through Piccadilly Circus. I knew the English team was due to be announced that day, and made use of the car radio to hear the glad news that I was in it.

So much for this digression on the announcement of international teams.

Although I was overjoyed to be playing for my country, especially at so early an age, my delight was tempered by a certain amount of foreboding. The reason was that Charlie Jones, my Highbury colleague and skipper, had already been chosen as right-half for the Welsh side. I realised that it would be doubly hard for me to impress. Charlie knew all my tricks and manoeuvres – probably better than I did myself! True, the right-back, and not he himself, would be directly responsible for my custody, but I knew Charlie's capacity for hard work well enough to realise that he would, at least, be a frequent visitor on my wing. If I had only realised how frequent, I would have spent some sleepless nights, before the day for the match arrived.

Apart from Charlie and myself, there was only one other Highbury representative among the twenty-two men who trotted out on to the Liverpool ground, at half-past two on a drab Wednesday afternoon. That was Bob John, who had been chosen as Wales' left-half. It was no less than Bob's fifth appearance against England, and the eleventh in his series of fourteen caps. The first of these, incidentally, had been gained while I was still at school!

The teams lined up as follows:

England: Hibbs (Birmingham); Cooper (Derby County); Blenkinsopp (Sheffield Wednesday); Strange (Sheffield Wednesday) (captain); Gee (Everton); Campbell (Huddersfield Town); Crooks (Derby County); Jack Smith (Portsmouth); Waring (Aston Villa); Hine (Leicester City); myself.

Wales: Gray (Tranmere Rovers); Williams (Everton) (captain); Ellis (Motherwell); Charlie Jones (Arsenal); Griffiths (Everton); John (Arsenal); Phillips (Wolves); O'Callaghan (Tottenham Hotspur); Astley (Aston Villa); Robbins (Cardiff City); Cook (Portsmouth).

I was deeply proud to be a member of an England side which included so many wonderful players. The peerless Harry Hibbs, the great full-back partnership of Tom Cooper and Tom Blenkinsopp, rivalled as an England combination only, perhaps, by Bob Crompton and Jesse Pennington, who went before them, or the all-Arsenal partnership of

Male and Hapgood, which was to be their successor; the great Alf Strange, who gained twenty international caps in his brilliant career – what an array of talent!

I had fellow-international debutants on the England side in centre-forward "Pongo" Waring, and centre-half-back Charlie Gee. An interesting feature of the match was that both centre-halves – Gee and Thomas – came from the same club. Gee had recently pushed Griffiths out of the Everton first team, and his displays had been so brilliant that he had attracted the attention of the English selectors. This was his reward.

The match itself was certainly an exciting one, and it must have been good to watch. I, personally, didn't enjoy it at all. The reason for my discomfort was – Charlie Jones. Charlie, who should by rights have been marking inside-left Ernie Hine, chose instead to cling to me like a bald-headed leech, throughout the whole of the game. I thought it most unfair. Of course, Charlie knew all my tactics practically off by heart, and what with this, his close marking, and the fact that I had right-back Williams looking after me as well, I had a thoroughly miserable game.

It was all very well as far as inside-left Ernie Hine was concerned. He often found himself left with a practically clear field, thanks to the unwelcome attentions which were being lavished on me, and enjoyed a successful game.

Unfortunately for me, the English selectors of those days were not particularly intelligent in their methods. With them, the emphasis always seemed to be laid on the individual performance of the player, rather than on how he fitted in with the team as a whole. It was a queer and unsatisfactory system, and I am glad that it does not obtain today.

Inspired by the magic of Ted Robbins, the Secretary of the Welsh F.A., Wales played with terrific dash and fire in the first half. They took the lead after thirty-one minutes' play, when Robbins, their inside-left, banged home a spectacular goal. But it was only three minutes before we were level.

Charlie Gee, who was a great success in this, his first international game, sent a long-distance free-kick into the Welsh goal mouth. The ball bounced off a Welsh defender to inside-right Jack Smith, who had it in the back of the net without further ado. Half-time came with no further score.

Somehow, it was not the same Wales in the second half; although it might well have been, so far as I was concerned. Sammy

Crooks put us ahead after six minutes' play, and twelve minutes later Ernie Hine made the game sure. His was an extremely well-taken goal. The ball came to him while he whipped round like lightening to flash it past Gray.

Ernie, as I have said, had quite a good game, but perhaps it was part due to him that I had such an undistinguished one myself. Unlike Alex James, who always stood well behind his centre-forward and winger, Ernie played well-up – and very close to me. I found this style of his disconcerting. When I wanted to cut inside, he would usually be in the way. If he had only stood farther towards the middle of the field, Charlie Jones would not have been able to mark me in the way he did. Alternatively, if he had done so, Ernie would have been in a position to take greater advantage of the open spaces which existed almost throughout the match, without his making best use of them.

Be that as it may, my international debut was not a happy one. I travelled back to London happy in the knowledge that I could now call myself a full-blown international, at the tender age of nineteen, but knowing full well that I was most unlikely to take an active role in England's next performance.

8
WE FALL BETWEEN TWO STOOLS

If 1930-31 had been a great season for Arsenal, 1931-32 promised at one period to be even greater. The coveted double – the achievement which had eluded every club in the full-scale modern football – seemed within our grasp. Then the walls of the castle we had been building in the air came tumbling down, and we at Highbury were left, dazed and disappointed, sitting among the ruins.

When the time came for the Third Round of the Cup, we were well placed in the League, and our Cup-tie opposition seemed to indicate that the luck was with us this season. We were drawn against Darwen, Champions of the Lancashire Combination, at Highbury.

As anticipated, it was a thoroughly one-sided game. We beat Darwen by the mammoth total of 11-1. This, so the newspapers told us, was the biggest Cup-tie win for twenty-six years. Be that as it may, I remember the game primarily not for our huge total, nor even the four goals I banged in myself, but for the grand sportsmanship of the Darwen players. They were totally outclassed, yet never did they show the slightest trace of resentment or ill-feeling; and never did they slacken in their efforts. Grand fellows that they were, they felt quite contented at having managed to penetrate the renowned Arsenal defence.

Outstanding on their side was Holden, a young inside-left. Herbert Chapman was so struck by his skill that he eventually brought him to Highbury. Alas, he was physically unsuited to the rigours of League Football, and never managed to make the grade.

We had a favourable draw in the next round, too – Plymouth Argyle, at home. Bill Harper, our former goalkeeper, was between the Plymouth posts, but he could not stop us recording a 4-2 win.

On to the Fifth Round – and this time we were away to Portsmouth: rather a tougher proposition than we had been faced with in the previous rounds. However, we took the obstacle in our stride, giving what I considered one of our best ever displays. There was never much question about the result.

I scored our first goal, in the first half – but I don't think I should have been allowed to score it. Alex James sent one of his long balls out to me, but Mackie, the Portsmouth and former Arsenal right-back, was there first. I was so far away from him that he had time enough to clear the ball twenty-five times over. He dallied, however, and I, always on the look-out for a chance, however slight, moved in towards him. The ball was running between Mackie and Gilfillan, the Portsmouth goalkeeper. So casual was Mackie that I was able to nip between the two of them, and get my toe to the ball just before Gilfillan. Arsenal were one up.

Joey Hulme obliged with a second, later in the game, and we were comfortably through to the Sixth Round, in which we were drawn away to Huddersfield Town. Meanwhile, we had been giving a very good account of ourselves in the League, and when the time came for the Huddersfield match we were lying second to Everton, one point behind and a game in hand. "Ah ha!" cries the self-styled expert, "you should have concentrated on the League!" This sounds all very well on the face of it. But there is a glamour about the Cup, to the footballer as well as the spectator, which transcends the workaday round of League warfare. The Arsenal attitude when well placed in the League at the turn of the year was, "Now let's have a crack at the double!" Greediness? Perhaps. But I myself consider that the chances of achieving this feat justify any risk that might be taken in the League.

We beat Huddersfield all right, but it was no easy task, and, strangely enough, we had centre-half Herbie Roberts to thank for the goal which gave us victory. Only two minutes of the game had elapsed when Herbie's ginger head popped up suddenly at a corner, and flashed the ball into the Huddersfield net. The Huddersfield players must have thought this rather unfair. I sympathise with them. After all, Herbie's job was stopping goals, not scoring them! This job he proceeded to carry out for the rest of the game, to such good intent that the full-time whistle saw us in our second Semi-Final in three seasons.

Manchester City were to provide the opposition. And it was no mean opposition, either. They had a team packed full of internationals: Matt Busby, the Scottish stylist, stalwart Sam Cowan, those dynamic Lancashire forwards Freddy Tilson and Eric Brook – they were foemen worthy of our steel, and I for one felt genuinely doubtful about the result. This is saying quite a lot. The Chapman spirit left very little room for doubt at Highbury.

As I feared, the City proved formidable opponents. They certainly enjoyed more of the play, but the mighty Arsenal defence withstood all their efforts to score. But we were not altogether sorry to see them doing more of the attacking – although at times it did seem too much of a good thing! – since it was Arsenal tactics to rely on sudden breakaway raids, more often than not instigated by a long pass from Alex James, the master schemer.

Eighty-nine out of the ninety minutes had gone by, and the score was still 0-0, when our defence at last managed to clear the ball after a seemingly endless spell of Manchester pressure. It came out to me, and I raced down the field as fast as I could. At about the half-way mark I sent a long pass out to the right wing. It was not a particularly accurate one, but Jack Lambert, one of whose greatest attributes was to chase any loose ball, dashed after it. It seemed a forlorn hope, however. Felton, the Manchester City left-back, had the ball well-covered, and decided to let it run out of play for a goal-kick. "He who hesitates is lost." Imagine Felton's surprise when Jack Lambert, giving a passable imitation of a steam engine, suddenly raced round him, and got his foot to the ball, a split second before it had crossed the goal-line.

Instinct had warned me to expect something like this. As Jack's centre came over, I was standing in the goal mouth ready to meet it. A shot; a gallantly ineffective dive by goalkeeper Langford, and the ball was in the Manchester net. Almost immediately, the final whistle blew, and Arsenal were at Wembley again.

Lucky Arsenal! I am not denying that Fortune smiled on us, in this game at St. Andrew's, Birmingham. On the run of play, City were the better team, and if Felton had only cleared, instead of letting the ball roll on, there might have been a very different story for the sports writers to tell. An amusing sideline on our win was that, just before I scored our goal, Herbert Chapman had fixed up with the Manchester City manager where the replay was going to be held!

Poor Manchester! But it is opportunism that wins cup-ties, and lion-hearted Jack Lambert's faithfulness to lost causes was responsible for the fact that Arsenal's red and not city's light blue was to be seen in the Final at Wembley. Jack's splendid low centre had given me an unmissable goal.

But if luck was on our side in the game against Manchester City, it certainly deserted us so far as the Final was concerned. Mainly responsible for our misfortune was the vast six-week gap between Semi-Final and Final. I contend that this gap is altogether too long. Far too much scope is given for injuries to the members of the Cup Final teams. Besides, with the Cup Final ahead, it is difficult for a team to give of its best in the League, and if it is in the running for both, as we were, the situation becomes doubly unfortunate.

Our Cup Final opponents-to-be, Newcastle United, met us in the "rehearsal", five weeks before the great game itself, in a League match at Highbury. We beat them 1-0 – not that it meant very much – thanks to a goal scored by Joey Hulme.

It was in another League game, against West Ham United, at Upton Park, that, to my mind, the Cup Final was virtually won and lost. For in that match Alex James was forced to leave the field, with a severely injured knee. Tom Whittaker worked desperately on him to get him fit for Wembley. For weeks, he was on the treatment-table at Highbury, and not until the Friday before the game did he come down to join the rest of us, in training at Brighton.

Every one of us gathered on the touch-lines of the Brighton and Hove Albion ground, and wee Alex was put through his test. All went well. The depression which had settled on everyone at Arsenal since his injury lifted for a few brief minutes. But Tom Whittaker was not satisfied; for Alex had not been subjected to a hard tackle. So on to the field came Alex again, the ball at his feet. A rugged interception by Tom – and there was the little Scotsman hobbling about in obvious agony.

Gloom descended on the team again. Going back to London in the train, Herbert Chapman called me aside. "You are going to play inside-left in the Final, Cliff," he said. I felt a little surprised, but honoured that he had picked on me to fill Alex's place. I was even more surprised when I learned that George Male was to be left-half, and Bob John outside left.

Chapman had made one of his very few mistakes. True, Bob John had been playing on the wing in recent matches, with some success. In our last game, he had scored twice against Sheffield Wednesday, while Portsmouth, incidentally, had thrashed Newcastle 6-0. But Bob was never really happy on the wing. True, again, my natural position was inside-left. But I had had very little experience there since I had come to Highbury. George Male's position at that time was at right and not left-half. This meant that Arsenal would be playing three men out of position.

To my mind, a more sensible reorganisation would have been to put George Male and Bob John in their natural positions at right and left-half respectively, while moving right-half Charlie Jones up to inside-left; the position in which he had joined Arsenal. Thus only one man, Charlie, would have been playing out of position – and this was one which he was well used to.

Well, what's done cannot be undone, as Lady Macbeth had pointed out, and Arsenal consequently lined up as follows:

Moss; Parker (captain); Hapgood; Jones; Roberts; Male; Hulme; Jack; Lambert; myself; John.

Newcastle United were represented by: McInroy; Nelson; Fairhurst; McKenzie; Davidson; Weaver; Boyd; Richardson; Allen; McMenemy and Lang.

We scored after fourteen minutes – yet, for once, the legend that the side scoring the first goal always wins the Final was to come unstuck. I started the movement which led to the goal, by putting Joe Hulme away, on the right wing. McInroy and Nelson, the Newcastle goalkeeper and right-back, both went for his high centre. They collided heavily, the ball came bouncing loose, and Bob John headed home. Pandemonium.

Newcastle drew level with their famous – infamous? – over-the-line goal, when Richardson chased a ball which seemed to roll well over the goal-line, and hooked it across for Allen to head into the net. I do not want to say very much about this incident, which has been discussed at length in many places. I will only state that the ball was undoubtedly over the line; to which assertion I add no qualifications; that the whole Arsenal defence stood still; and that the goal had a thoroughly disheartening effect on the whole of the Arsenal team, myself included. It was not just a case of perhaps the ball was over the line, perhaps it was not. We all knew quite well it had gone out of play. So, apparently, did everyone, except the referee.

Allen scored again in the second half, and we had lost. Yet, although we were a shadow of the team we could be with Alex James' inspiration, we had enough chances to have at least forced a draw. David Jack, who played at centre-forward in the second half, with Jack Lambert at inside-left and myself at inside-right, missed when he only had to tap the ball into an open goal.

It was not our day. In fact, it was not our season. Second to Everton, six points behind, when the Final came, we subsequently made up four points of the leeway, to finish with fifty-four to their fifty-six. Yet if we had won the Final, I am convinced we would have won the League as well.

Second in the Championship, Runners-up in the F.A. Cup: that was our lot in season 1931-32. A little more luck, and we might have triumphed in both. As it was, we gained neither. Such, I suppose, is life. We never came so near to the double again.

9
THE GREATNESS OF TOM WHITTAKER

During the course of my football career I met hundreds of different personalities, from all walks of life; famous and obscure, great and insignificant. For none of them did I have greater respect and admiration than for Tom Whittaker.

I did not come into contact with Tom very much when I first arrived at Highbury. Not being a regular first-team player, I had my peg in the second eleven dressing-room, and was trained and looked after by Billy Milne; now, of course, Arsenal's senior trainer. Midway through the season, however, a place in the first team dressing-room was mine, and Tom became responsible for my fitness and well-being.

The first thing that struck me about Tom, even before I came to know him well, was his extreme youthfulness for a man in his responsible position. Indeed, he was younger than several of the players he trained. Tom once remarked, "It has often been said that I am too young to be the trainer of a first-class club; but the grand set of boys I have to look after makes life easy for me." This was typical of Tom – passing the credit on to others than himself.

Solidly built, Tom, at this stage of his career, almost always seemed to have a worried expression on his face; he took his responsibilities very seriously. Yet he was modest in the extreme, and few appeared less impressed by his astonishing healing powers than himself. Shy and modest he was, Tom nevertheless had a smile which could put me at my ease, and fill me with a glow of confidence. I always felt there was something paternal about it and him.

He became trainer in a rather curious way. He was, of course, a player for Arsenal, and at the end of the 1924-25 season he was chosen to go on the Football Association tour of Australia. While there he was unlucky enough to sustain a knee injury, which terminated his playing career, long before its natural end.

Herbert Chapman took Tom on to the training side at Highbury, with that kindly regard for the welfare of his players which was always one of his chief characteristics. One day, George Hardy, then the Arsenal trainer, did something of which Chapman severely disapproved. Without a moment's delay, Chapman went straight to Tom Whittaker, and told him: "Tom, you are going to be the Arsenal trainer!"

Tom was flabbergasted. In vain he protested his inexperience, his youth and his lack of medical knowledge. It was of no avail. Chapman's mind was made up, and all Tom's objections – cogent as they were – were swept aside like straws before a waterfall.

What magnificent foresight Chapman possessed! Tom became the greatest trainer football has ever known – and probably the greatest attached to any sport whatsoever, for that matter.

Tom, as I have already remarked, was very young indeed, to be the trainer of a first-class side. Yet he was so natural and unaffected, in spite of his great surgical gifts, and the skill in applying them which he had acquired, since the day Chapman dropped his bombshell, that none of the players resented his command.

I sensed his authority over them almost as soon as I came to Arsenal. Tom did not have to tell players under his command what to do. So great was our respect for him, that we did it automatically. No club could have been more enthusiastic about its training than we were, under Tom. Although it was not the fashion among other clubs, we used to train five days a week. There was no obligation for us to come in on a Monday, at all. Nevertheless, everybody did. Friday – which was a compulsory day – was also not generally observed among Football League teams. But I never heard any player complain.

Tom's healing powers were truly phenomenal. People from all walks of life came to the Arsenal Stadium for treatment under his magic hands. One was Bernard Gadney, the famous Rugby International. He came down to Highbury on crutches, so grave was the extent of his injury. Some of the most eminent surgeons in London had assured him that his playing days were over. He came to Tom as a last, desperate effort. The following year, he was captain of the England Rugby team.

Tom was always a great friend to me personally. I can never thank him enough for the care and expert treatment he lavished on me, whilst I was at Highbury. Perhaps "expert" is a badly chosen word; for Tom was something more than an expert. There was about him a touch of genius.

To him, as much as any man, was due the amazing success enjoyed by Arsenal between the two World Wars. Men who, under any other pair of hands, would have remained on the injured list for three or four weeks, Tom would have fit again in three or four days. And besides, there was the keenness to train which he succeeded in inspiring all us players.

Yet all roads led to Herbert Chapman – at least, so far as Arsenal were concerned. Tom's road leads there, too. Without Chapman, it is more than probable that his great natural gifts would never have achieved realisation.

A few little anecdotes of how Tom helped me, during my Highbury career, may serve to illustrate what I mean. Thanks to my journeys with English and Football League international sides – of which Tom was not always the trainer – I was able, during my playing days to study the methods of almost all the famous English trainers. None even approached the same class as Tom.

Once, I tore a muscle in my leg. It was that which controlled the foot, and, as if this wasn't bad enough – my left foot, the foot which made me famous. I was quite unable to control its movements. It hung at the end of my leg, limp and useless as a deflated balloon.

Tom took the situation in hand. He bound that foot with yards of plaster, twisting deviously this way and that. And that Saturday, I played. Tom, in effect, had manufactured me an artificial muscle!

On another occasion he again came to the rescue, when all seemed helplessly lost. Arsenal had been playing a match in the north, the first in a three in three days Christmas series. We arrived back in London late at night, and went back to Highbury for hot baths, to ease out our stiffness, in preparation for the coming day's game. I undressed, went into the bathroom, and put my foot into the bath. It didn't stay there long. The water was positively scalding. My foot only remained in it for a split second, but that was quite long enough to bring about an enormous blister. Tom took the matter in hand at once. He applied ointment, and swathed the foot in bandages, but even these measures could not entirely allay the intense pain I was suffering.

After he had attended to me, Tom had a few crisp words for the man who had been responsible for running the bath. The fellow was bitterly upset, and wept copiously. He swore vehemently that he believed he had run cold water into the bath. Obviously, it was nothing but an unhappy mistake. This, however, did not give any relief to my throbbing foot.

That night we slept in a London hotel. At least, some of the players may have done. I know I didn't. I was in positive agony the whole night, and nobody could have felt less like playing in a football match than I, the following morning.

"How do you feel?" Tom asked me, when he came into my bedroom before we left for Highbury. I told him. "Never mind, Cliff," said Tom, "I can fix you up."

"Well, Tom," I answered, "you know I want to go home to Exeter for a few days, after Christmas. If I don't play today, I shall have to stay at Highbury for treatment. If you can get me into anything approaching proper condition, I'll play."

Believe it or not, I played! With the skill that was all his own, Tom so bandaged and padded my injured foot that I was able to squeeze it into my football boot – kick the ball as hard as I pleased, with no ill effects. Pain was non-existent. The only intimation I had that the blister was there was – excuse me – the feel, when I moved, of the water inside it running up and down my foot.

Ultimately, it burst. I had just kicked the ball at a corner, when it did so. Incidentally, we won that game, as we won all three, that Christmas. We went on to win the League that season, as well.

I am quite convinced that no other trainer in football could have done what Tom Whittaker did for me that day.

But perhaps the most interesting story about Tom and myself concerns a point rather higher up on my leg – my knee. I was training by myself at the back of the Arsenal Stadium, on a spring day in 1935, when suddenly my left knee went out of joint. I limped into the ground itself, and informed Tom Whittaker of the fact. At first, Tom would not believe me. At length, however, he credited my story, fiddled with the knee for a few minutes, and finally succeeded in coaxing it back into place. Before that knee had finished troubling me, Tom had done this for me at least twenty times.

For the next few weeks, the snap of that knee became an all too familiar sound. I did not drop out of the team, however, and some weeks later, just before the England team to meet Scotland was due to be chosen, I lined up with the Arsenal team at Villa Park. All was rosy, we were beating the Villa by three goals to one, and I was enjoying a successful game, when, a few minutes from time....Yes, you've guessed it: the knee went.

Tom carried me off the field into the Arsenal dressing-room, and began fiddling it back into place. It was rather like juggling with a combination lock. Indeed, ever since my knee trouble, combination locks have received my heartfelt sympathy.

By the time my knee was back in position the game was over, so there was no need or opportunity to go back on the field again, and put it to the test. Attending the match was Mr. Rinder, a member of the Football Association selection committee, which, of course, chooses all the England teams. I was likely to be chosen as England's inside-right against Scotland, at Hampden Park, the following Monday, and was greatly looking forward to my first experience of the formidable Hampden Roar. Consequently, when Mr. Rinder anxiously enquired of me whether I would be all right if selected for the Scotland game, I gave him a definite affirmative. After all, when the knee did go wrong it only took a few minutes to put back; and there were no after-effects. Besides it was going to take a very serious injury, indeed, to deprive me of a cap against Scotland.

On the journey up to Glasgow for the game, the following week, Mr. Harry Huband, another of the England selectors, who was, of course, accompanying the England party, seemed rather dubious of my fitness. Yet curiously enough his suspicions centred, not on my knee, but on my shoulder! Why he entertained these forebodings I do not know, unless I happened to be holding my arm in a peculiar position, on some occasion when he was watching me. Certainly, there was nothing wrong with my shoulder. But there was still plenty wrong with my leg!

Twenty minutes or so of the international had gone by, when Bob McPhail, the Scottish inside-left and I jumped together for a high ball. Quite incidentally, Bob's knee touched mine as we rose into the air. The inevitable happened. It promptly went out of joint.

Tom Whittaker, who, luckily for me, was England trainer for the occasion, had strapped up the knee with bandages and hope, before the game began. Now he ran out on to the field and manoeuvred it into place again.

All well and good – or so it appeared. But by now, however, I felt really scared that another knock on the knee would mean good-bye to international football. Consequently, I was afraid to turn sharply Of course, this had a most unfavourable effect on my play.

After the match – which we lost 2-0, thanks to a couple of Dally Duncan goals – the sports writers raised a cry of "England played unfit men." Maybe I should not really have taken the risk of letting England down, but....what would you have done?

After the international was over, I was besieged by a host of enquiring reporters. What was wrong with my leg? Was it serious?

Would I be able to play again that season? I wished I knew the answers to those questions myself.

I went back with Tom Whittaker to his bedroom, in the hotel where the England party was staying. "Well, Tom," I said, "tell me the worst. What do you think about it?" But for one of the few occasions in his life Tom Whittaker was baffled. "I don't know what to think," he said. "There's no swelling, so it certainly can't be cartilage." At that moment, in walked Mr. George Allison, our secretary-manager, in succession to Herbert Chapman.

"Cheer up, Cliff," he said, "you'll play next Saturday, all right. Come downstairs and have a champagne cocktail!"

"That's all very well, Mr. Allison," I relied; "no doubt I shall be fit to play on Saturday, but the whole thing's gone too far, now. It's high time something was done about it."

Accordingly, Mr. Allison arranged as appointment for me with one of the foremost osteopaths in Britain; a titled man, a knight, whose name was, and still is, a household word. Although he had enjoyed huge success, he was frowned on by more orthodox members of the medical profession, but this had no effect on his popularity. He had about him a bluff, breezy manner, and he was certainly far from being his own worst enemy.

He sat me down on a chair, and fiddled about with my knee for a few minutes. "I know what's wrong with you," he said. "The knee is out of line. Protruding cartilage and strained ligaments." He took hold of my leg again, manipulated it this way and that for a while, and then pronounced the cartilage to be in line once more.

I paid him several more visits, until, one day, he told me that I was fit to play the following Saturday. "And if the cartilage does come out again," he said nonchalantly, "you'll have to visit me at my villa in Spain, for further treatment." He resided in Spain for most of the year, only coming back to see patients as a special favour.

As a matter of interest, when Mr. Allison subsequently enquired of him the extent of his fee, he replied that it usually ran into the neighbourhood of a thousand guineas. As he had been a shareholder of Arsenal, however, he was willing to waive it completely on this occasion.

A few days before my leg was put to the test, I went with the other members of the Arsenal first team to play golf, at the Old Ford Manor Club. After we had finished our round, Mr. Allison called me into the clubhouse, for a cup of tea. "You've seen Sir____, Cliff," he said. "Physically, there is nothing wrong with you now. All you've got to do is settle yourself mentally about the knee, as well."

"Frankly, Mr. Allison," I said, I can't see what he's done for me. But anyway, we shall see."

Tom Whittaker shared my opinion. "If that knee of yours is all right, Cliff," he said, "then I don't know my job."

Accordingly, then, I trotted out on to the field at Highbury the following Saturday; hopeful, but – I confess it – doubtful, too. My doubts were fully justified. Shortly after half time, I heard a painfully familiar snap – and the knee had gone again. Tom Whittaker, disappointed, but not surprised, carried me off the field. Mr. Allison was waiting for him at the trainer's bench. "Well, Tom, he said, "did it go out?"

"Of course it did," said Tom shortly. "Why do you think I was out there all that time?"

Mr. Allison looked positively flabbergasted. "I don't understand it," he said.

This was not really very surprising. I went to a variety of eminent specialists in London, and they could not understand it, either. One of them, hoping for the best, slapped a plaster on my leg, to bring up the fluid which he thought – somewhat hopefully, perhaps – was causing all the trouble. The plaster took effect while I was resting at my Exeter home.

Before I left Highbury, I had received instructions to return to London for further treatment, as soon as this should happen. Accordingly, I was climbing into my car, thinking wishfully that the days of my knee trouble were over, when – need I say it – the wretched thing went out of position again.

"Mother," I called, "my leg's gone." My mother rushed downstairs at once. "Now, Mother," I said, "I want you to do just as I tell you." Then as nearly as I could remember, I tried to show her how to put the knee back, the way Tom Whittaker had done. "I'm no Tom Whittaker," Mother complained. All her efforts were of no avail. I remained a temporary cripple.

I telephoned to the Arsenal Stadium for instructions. They told me to have the knee put back into place again, and come back to London for attention. I tried four doctors in Exeter, to have the knee put back. Of the first three, two found the task beyond them, whilst the third did not want to take the risk of trying. One of them, after fiddling unsuccessfully with the knee, told me he could force it back – but I would have to have a dose of chloroform. I declined.

Finally, I tried a friend's local doctor, who came to visit me at my home. If efforts alone brought results, he would have put my leg back into position ten times over. For two hours he struggled with it. At the end of this period he looked as if he had just come out of a Turkish bath. But he might as well have saved his strength. The knee stayed as it was.

I was saved further torment at the hands of the medicos of Exeter when a telephone call came through from Highbury, ordering me to return to London at once, whether he leg was out of position or not. I left Exeter immediately, and was met in London by Tom Whittaker and Dr. Pepper, the club doctor. They took me at once to a specialist.

The specialist diagnosed that it was cartilage trouble, and that I would have to undergo an operation. "Sooner than have an operation, I'll pack up the game", I said. Although I was only twenty-three years old at the time, and thus had many more seasons in front of me, I was fully in earnest when I made this startling decision. I have always had a curious inexplicable dread of hospitals and operations, and preferred to give up the game I loved, rather than take the risk of becoming a helpless cripple for the rest of my life.

Tom Whittaker, however, persuaded me that the operation was in my best interests, and I at length agreed to have it. I always took Tom's advice, however much it might go against my own prejudices and opinions. Accordingly, I was wheeled into an operating theatre for the first time in my life.

Everything happened to me. Let the words of the *British Medical Journal* describe just what a state my left knee was in: *"On opening the joint slight excess of dark-coloured synovial fluid escaped. The lesion was clearly a longitudinal tear of a disc-shaped semilunar cartilage, or what in the case of cartilage of the usual type would be designated a bucket-handled lesion. In this case, however, the "handle", or inner portion, was prolonged internally in the form of a broad web-like extension, into which haemorrhage had occurred. The specimen has been accepted by the Museum of the Royal College of Surgeons."* So if the football world doesn't remember me in future years, at least the medical world will!

The extract from the *British Medical Journal* above is, as a matter of interest, reproduced from a pamphlet entitled *The Disc-shaped External Semilunar Cartilage*, which was sent to me with the compliments of the author, who thought the essay significant enough to republish in separate form.

While I was convalescing after the operation, the surgeon who had performed it came to see what progress I was making. He was full of praise for Tom Whittaker, who had attended at the operation, and had assisted him in various ways.

"Tom was magnificent!" he said. "You should have thought he'd been in an operating theatre every day of his life. I wanted to come to an arrangement with him, under which I performed operations, and he helped me to look after the patients, while they were convalescing. He refused, though: it's a great pity. I'm positive we could make a fortune together, that way."

What a tribute to Tom! What other football trainer could have distinguished himself in the operating theatre as he did, that day?

Luckily for me, the operation was a complete success. By the time the next season began I was perfectly fit, and regained my place in the Arsenal and England teams.

In 1947 Tom Whittaker was appointed manager of Arsenal, in succession to Mr. George Allison. I was very happy when I heard the news. I felt Tom was the only man who could revive the Chapman tradition – a tradition which had been broken under George Allison, but which now was certain to come into its own again.

10
WHO WAS WHO AT HIGHBURY

I have already said a good deal of Herbert Chapman and Tom Whittaker, manager and trainer of Arsenal when I joined the club from Exeter. In this chapter, I want to say something of the men who were my colleagues in the mighty Arsenal teams of the Chapman era. Some of them, of course, were with me in the Allison era, too.

Captain and right-back, until he lost his place to George Male early in season 1932-33 was Tom Parker. Temperamentally, Tom was the last person to skipper a team. Far from being the cool, firm, steady type, he was one of the most nervous footballers I have ever met. He would go through agonies before a game began, and nobody would be more happy than he when it eventually started. Once the ball had been kicked off, Tom's nervousness would disappear, and for the rest of the afternoon he would be imperturbability itself. Tom, who took very seriously his duties as captain, would make brave efforts to maintain an unruffled demeanour in the dressing-room; but one could always sense the undercurrents of uncertainty which lurked beneath.

Apart from his temperament, however, Tom made an ideal captain. He was a thoroughgoing gentleman, and his behaviour was always an example to the rest of the team, both on and off the field. Never have I known a footballer more loyal to his club, and more wholehearted in his efforts to serve it.

As a footballer, he was a very useful man to have in one's team, but he never achieved football greatness. His greatest strength lay in his uncanny positional sense. His bald head was like a magnet for passes by the opposite side. Goodness knows how many times that head saved Arsenal in a nasty situation. Tom, however, was not a great all-round back. His play lacked polish, and he was not well versed in the finer points of the game.

Far different was the case of his partner at left-back, Eddie Hapgood. Eddie, like Tom Parker a total abstainer, was the finest full-back I have ever seen. Even when I first came to Highbury, when Eddie was but twenty years old, he bore the stamp of greatness. Eddie had football developed into a meticulously exact science. His method of tackling was all his own. Never would you see him rush at an opponent, hoping blindly for the best. If he did decide that a tackle was necessary, he would wait carefully until exactly the right moment, and then....presto: the ball was at his feet.

Allied to his tackling skill was a positional sense every bit as good as Tom Parker's, and the ability to kick with equal power and accuracy either with the right or the left foot. This is a very rarely seen attribute, especially among defenders. Eddie was one of the few men I played with or against who possessed it.

Ask any winger who played against him, and they will tell you that he was infinitely harder to beat than the back who crashes in to the tackle, like a charging rhinoceros. Eddie besides all this, was terrifically enthusiastic, and possessed a wonderful fighting spirit. He was, indeed, and ideal captain, and fully deserved the honour of captaining England, which fell to him on so many occasions. Eddie never caused the slightest trouble, on or off the field. A foul against him was a rarity. Indeed, his cultured style of play could hardly have made it anything else.

His mannerisms, on and off the field of play, led to an impression in some quarters that he suffered from a swollen head. Even if he had, there would have been plenty of reason for him to have done so, but in point of fact this impression was absolutely groundless. Eddie and I have known each other for many years, and, as England players, have travelled all over Europe together. I could not have wished for a pleasanter or more modest travelling companion.

Eddie's partner, in succession to Tom Parker, was, of course, George Male. What a magnificent pair these two made! They partnered each other in the England team on no less than fourteen occasions. Both captained the national side, while, including wartime honours, they collected between them no less than sixty-eight England and Football League caps. What a record!

George came to Arsenal from the Isthmian League amateur club, Clapton, in 1930. But he did not come as a full-back; he came, believe it or not, as a left-half. It was there that he made his Arsenal debut, in 1930, and it was there that he played, as a last minute choice, in the Cup Final of 1932. How he came to switch from the one position to the other makes another Herbert Chapman story.

On another autumn day in 1933 Mr. Chapman suddenly decided that Arsenal needed a new right-back. Tom Parker was at the end of his tether, and obviously needed to be replaced. Chapman had young George Male – he was twenty-two years old, at the time – sent up to his office, and dropped yet another of his bombshells. "George," he announced, "you are going to become a right-back." Before George could open his mouth in a gasp, Chapman had already begun to give him a strong dose of the hypnotic eloquence which I have never seen equalled, before or since. "By the time I got out of that room," George told me afterwards, "I wasn't only convinced that I was a full-blown right-back, I knew without doubt that I was the best right-back in the country!"

How did Chapman come to these remarkable decisions? He could take enough blood out of a stone to fill a large-sized swimming-bath. George Male at the time was, with all due deference to him, just an undistinguished reserve wing-half. He developed into the best right-back Arsenal have ever had, and worked up an understanding with Eddie Hapgood which made them the finest pair of club backs in the country; probably the finest in the world. Indeed, he lived up to all Chapman prophesied for him. Chapman! Was he a man, or a magician?

George Male perhaps lacked Eddie Hapgood's polish. He had positional sense which was not a jot behind Eddie's, however, while his powers of recovery were considerable. George was rather the Tom Parker than the Eddie Hapgood type of back, but he was a far more accomplished player than Tom – which is saying a good deal.

Temperamentally, George was rather like myself. Quiet and retiring, with very little to say for himself, his success never impaired his modesty.

Behind these full-backs was, for a few years at least, goalkeeper Frank Moss. Like most goalkeepers, Frank was a little crazy. One has to be, to take the risks those fellows take. I have driven in Frank's car on occasions, and wished very heartily I was elsewhere, as we twisted and turned through the traffic as terrifying speed.

As a footballer, we never saw the best of Frank. If an injury to his shoulder had not cut short his career, I am convinced he would have become the greatest keeper of all time. Certainly, I rank him with the best I ever saw – and that is not just Arsenal prejudice. Frank had an uncanny sense of anticipation. He always seemed to know what an oncoming forward was going to do. I think this talent of his was attributable to the fact that he often played as a forward in our practice games, when he always showed ball control which was more than good enough for a First Division forward – let alone a goalkeeper!

Frank always prided himself on his ability as a forward, and had a chance to display it, when he played what turned out to be his last match in first-class football: against Everton, at Goodison Park.

Switched to the left wing, after an injury to that wretched shoulder of his, he scored Arsenal's equalising goal, when all seemed lost. After he had been medically advised that he would never play as a goalkeeper again, he was convinced that he would be able to stay in first-class football as a forward. However, this whim of his never came to anything, and he subsequently became manager of Hearts.

I know there will be strong challenges, when I say that Frank was the most accomplished goalkeeper I ever saw, but I stand by my statement, nevertheless. Allied to his sense of anticipation was agility, fearlessness, and the ability to kick readily and powerfully with either foot. Most goalkeepers are restricted entirely to one foot, for goal-kicks and clearances. Not so Frank.

I can hear a low, angry murmur from the Black Country: "What about Harry Hibbs?" Harry, I know, is generally ranked, today, as the greatest goalkeeper of all time. I cannot coincide with this opinion. For this dissension from general opinion, I have what I consider very good reasons. Firstly, Harry, like Tom Parker, was the nervous type of player. Both, if they started the game on the wrong foot, were liable to go from bad to worse. Both never rid themselves of this unfortunate weakness, although they spent many years in the highest classes of football. If Harry Hibbs made a save or two, early in a match, he would in all probability play like a superman for the remainder of the ninety minutes. If, on the other hand, he let through an early goal, other goals were more than likely to follow.

My second quarrel against Harry, as a goalkeeper, is that he punched the ball far too much. Punching does not make for accuracy, and is at the best of times a risky business. A goalkeeper who indulges too much in this habit is likely to find himself beaten by a first-time volley, before he has time to recover his balance and position.

But let us return from Harry Hibbs to Arsenal – that is, if my Birmingham readers will bear with me any longer! Arsenal's wing-halves formed a fascinating contrast in character; though so far as actual style of play was concerned they were roughly similar. Both were Welsh; both were internationals. They were, in fact, Charlie Jones and Bob John.

Charlie Jones took over the captaincy of Arsenal from Tom Parker. He had come to Arsenal from Nottingham Forest, as an inside-left. Subsequently, he became an outside-left, and then, when I had taken over on the left wing, a right-half.

Charlie was one of the gentlemen of football. Reserved and thoughtful, he took the game very seriously, and was always working out new schemes, whereby his own play or the play of the team could be benefited. He was thoughtful on the field, too; always trying to see a couple of moves ahead – and often succeeding, too. This thoughtfulness, allied to his sound tackling, made up for his lack of weight and inches.

As a skipper of Arsenal, Charlie once became rather unpopular, through his insistence on one of his plans. This was the scheme of "man for man", whereby each player was responsible for one opponent, and, virtually, one opponent only. If that man got the ball, then the Arsenal man responsible for him must give chase until the opponent in question was dispossessed, or had parted with the ball. This was all very well up to a point – and up to a point, Arsenal always played thus. But if this scheme was too meticulously applied, it led to the disruption of the covering system, which was the secret of Arsenal's defensive solidity. It took quite a while to persuade Charlie to drop this scheme, but eventually, drop it he did.

Charlie was always studying something. At one period, it was algebra, I remember. During a railway trip up north, for an away match, he came upon a most intriguing little problem, which David Jack decided he would try to solve. David, one of the most well educated footballers there has ever been, a man conversant, thanks to his job, with all the manifold mysteries of Inland Revenue, covered sheet after sheet of paper, in a vain endeavour to solve the elusive problem. "Let me have a try," said Tom Whittaker.

Within two minutes, Tom had the problem correctly solved! It is largely thanks to my acquaintanceship with Tom Whittaker that I resist the definition of genius as "an infinite capacity for taking pains".

Left-half Bob John was the most unassuming man I have ever met. If I was quiet in my ways, then Bob was a veritable oyster. He used to say, with a pointed glance at earnest Charlie Jones, that one Welsh talker in the club was enough! Bob was one of the finest footballers I ever came across, yet so unspectacular – almost unobtrusive – was his style of play, that he never received the credit he deserved.

I was very, very lucky to have Bob playing behind me, during my first seasons at Highbury. His shrewd prompting was calculated to bring the best out of any winger, while he won so many tackles that the amount of balls he was able to send up to his forwards was prodigious.

Bob's coolness was amazing: so was his control of the ball. He had a knack of bringing a ball down to his feet from mid-air, instead of waiting for it to hit the ground, before trapping it, as most players do. I have seen him bring the ball to his feet like this, oh, so coolly, even in the midst of his own crowded penalty area – or his opponents'. One final tribute to Bob. Never once, in all the years I knew him, did I see him play a bad game.

Between Bob and Charlie, guarding the centre of the field, was big, red-headed Herbie Roberts – another of football's gentlemen. Herbie, taciturn and unassuming, was a terrific tackler, and made such use of his height that he was practically unbeatable when the ball was in the air. As an all-round player he may have had his failings, but he fitted in perfectly with the Arsenal scheme of things. Besides, he was not altogether unconstructive, as many people would have you believe.

Seldom was it that he wasted a ball. Alex James picked up ball after ball from him in midfield, while I, too, received plenty of fine passes from him.

Now and again, Herbie would come into the goal-scoring, as opposed to the goal-preventing, picture. There was the time when he won a Sixth Round cup-tie for us, at Huddersfield, by heading a beautiful goal from a corner. That was in 1932. I recall him getting another for us at Derby, in 1930, when the County broke our non-stop undefeated League run. And another, sadder occasion, when Herbie twice put through his own goal, in the space of a few minutes, during a match against Derby County, at Highbury.

Poor Herbert. He died during the war from erysipelas, a Captain in the Royal Fusiliers, and still a young man.

What about my colleagues in the forward line? The most colourful of them all – with one obvious exception – was outside-right Joey Hulme. Temperamentally, Joey was rather of the Tom Parker type. In spite of many seasons' experience in top-class football, he never could rid himself of nervous qualms before a match. This nervousness often manifested itself in outbreaks of practical joking. Joe was certainly the Arsenal humorist, but his fooling was largely designed, I feel, to cover up and drive away his nervous misgivings.

I have already recounted the prank he played at Brighton, on poor Charlie Preedy. One other escapade is, I think, well worth the telling. Joe arrived one morning at the Arsenal Stadium for training, carrying in his hand the bowl of a clay pipe. "This," he said, to the crowd of curious players, including myself, which had gathered around him, "is a coffin and this," taking a lighted cigarette end from his mouth, "is the man inside it."

So saying, Joe popped the cigarette end inside the pipe bowl, and stood it upside down on the table in front of him. "I'm willing to bet anybody any money they like," he announced, "that when I take the coffin away, the dead man inside will still be standing up." Joey then turned aside to borrow a box of matches from somebody's coat, which was hanging on the wall. As he did so, Jack Campbell, the head of our ground staff, who was standing by, surreptitiously took the cigarette end from underneath the pipe-bowl.

Joe, who had had his back turned while this neat little robbery was taking place, now returned to the table, and, with meticulous care, began to arrange his matches in neat lines around the pipe-bowl. "This," he said solemnly, "is the tombstone. Now, how about those bets?"

Any bookmaker might have felt jealous of the business Joey did, in the course of the next few minutes. He was never particularly free with his money, and every one of us laid a bet, longing for the look of surprise which would cover Joe's face when he found the trick which had been played on him. The bets all having been carefully noted down, Joe made a few "magic" passes over the pipe-bowl, muttered several mystic words – then carefully raised it.

Underneath was – a glowing cigarette end!

"Let that be a lesson to you all," said Joey severely. "This time, you can all have your money back – next time I shan't be so generous!"

What had actually happened was that Joey had met Jack Campbell on his way into the Stadium, and had carefully instructed him in his role of conjuror's assistant. Although Jack had filched one cigarette end, another was carefully fixed inside the clay bowl!

As a footballer, Joey was one of the best outside-rights I have ever known. Yet he could also be one of the worst. His nervousness sometimes made him play far, far below his normal form. Indeed, Joe could at times look more like an amateur than an English International.

Yet when his nerves were not bothering him – and it was only occasionally that he suffered from them – Joe's lightening speed and astonishing ball control were far too much for almost any back. He had, too, a knack of putting over centres, often at top speed, which I have never seen rivalled for their accuracy. Once, I saw him give a display in an international trial at Portsmouth, which I rank as the finest exhibition of wing play it was ever my privilege to witness. Joe was marked that afternoon by the classic Ernie Blenkinsop, so he had no mean opposition to contend with. But Ernie was never in the picture. I'm sure he never will forget that game. The only way he – or anybody else – could have stopped Joey was by digging a couple of man-traps. The funny thing about it was that Joey only came into the trial as a third reserve. Yet so brilliant was his performance that the selectors just had no alternative but to cap him in the match against Scotland.

Every game came easily to Joe. He was a first-class cricketer, playing many years for Middlesex. One day he was batting at Lord's against Learie Constantine, the West Indian "demon" bowler. Several balls came whistling down, none of which Joe had time even to lift his bat to. At last, after another delivery, the umpire called, "No ball!"

"So that's what it is," said Joe, "I knew something funny was going on!"

Joe thought nothing of making a century break at billiards. He decided to take up golf, and within a few months was one of the best players at Highbury. This, mind you, was at a time when Arsenal could have put out a team of Walker Cup standard.

Joey's partner, most of the time he was at Highbury, was tall, impeccably-dressed David Jack. David, who came to Arsenal from Bolton, with a great reputation which he proceeded to enhance, was probably the best-educated Soccer professional of his day. Such a dandy was he in his dress, that he would arrive for a football match wearing spats! This craze spread for a time to the whole Arsenal team.

David, always a trifle aloof in his manner, took a great deal of getting to know. But once you could get underneath his rather cold exterior, you had found a friend very well worth having.

David was one of the finest attacking inside-rights I ever saw. As such, he made an ideal complement to the scheming Alex James. An amazing natural body swerve and a terrific shot made him a terror to defences. But he was essentially a one-wing player, and I, as outside-left to his inside-right, could count on one hand the number of passes I received from him in any single game.

Jack Lambert, our crashing centre-forward, was one of the finest whole-hearted players I have ever seen. Many people label Jack as a mere crasher, asserting that any centre-forward placed between a couple of inside men like David Jack and Alex James just could not help getting goals. I disagree with this point of view entirely.

No one can deny that Jack was blessed with a ball service which has probably never been afforded to any other centre-forward, before or since. Nevertheless, he didn't always get the ball placed right on his toe or head, practically asking to be put into the net. More often he would have to go racing hell-for-leather down the field, with an assorted collection of enemy half-backs and full-backs tearing, wolf-like, at his heels. And even when he had outstripped them, there was still the goalkeeper to come. True, a forward bearing down on goal with only the goalie to beat is presented with a big advantage. But how often does one see that advantage abused? Few forwards have used it more often and more efficiently than Jack.

Jack had skill, too. A goal he scored at Upton Park, in a Cup-tie against West Ham, provides a good example of that. He swerved and dribbled half the length of the field, and finally walked the ball into the net. I considered him exceptionally unlucky not to have gained an England cap in the 1930-31 season, when goals flowed from his boot and head with almost monotonous consistency. Had any other centre-forward than the great Dixie Dean been in circulation at the time, Jack would surely have gained his just reward.

On several occasions, Chapman brought centre-forwards of great reputation and greater expense to Highbury, in order to get a more polished leader for the Arsenal attack. But every time the lot finally came back to rest upon the broad, strong shoulders of Jack Lambert. Jimmy Dunne, George Hunt, Davie Halliday, Tim Coleman – none of them could keep him out of the Arsenal side for very long.

Jack scored goals galore for Arsenal, but I shall always remember one particular feat of his. This took place on Christmas Eve, 1932, at Highbury. Arsenal smashed Sheffield United by nine goals to two, and Jack accomplished the greatest performance of his career by netting five of them. Poor Jack. He was killed in a road accident, early in the recent war, when he was managing the Arsenal nursery. His loss was a severe one to football, but even severer to those who knew him well.

Amid this galaxy of Arsenal stars which I have just been recalling, one name is very conspicuous by its absence. The name, of course, if that of Alex James. But do not fret, dear readers. I have left him out entirely on purpose. For Alex must have a chapter to himself.

Arsenal team, season 1934-35.

England *versus* Hungary, 1934.

A famous forward line: Hulme, Jack, Colman, James, Bastin.

England team versus Ireland, at Stoke, November 1936.

Arsenal's three internationals: Hapgood, Bastin, Copping.

Training at Highbury: Hapgood, Bastin, Copping, Tom Whittaker.

Cliff Bastin with other members of the team in the dressing-room.

A picture taken in between filming shots for *"The Arsenal Stadium Mystery"*.

11
MY PARTNERSHIP WITH ALEX JAMES

As a personality and as a footballer, Alex James was quite in a class of his own. On and off the field, he was a law unto himself – although off it he sometimes found himself guided into more orthodox paths by Mr. Herbert Chapman. There is no doubt that Alex will always be remembered, as long as football is played. I count myself lucky to have played beside him, forming the Alex James – "Boy" Bastin wing which gained so much publicity, in the pre-war days of Arsenal's success.

When I first met Alex, he was an established player, a Scottish International, who had come to Arsenal for the huge fee, for those days, of £9,000. The only similarity between us was that we had both been signed as inside-lefts, during the close season of 1929. I realised at once that Alex would be first choice in the Arsenal team for that position, but since he was more than a decade older than I was, I reckoned my chance would ultimately come. That it was eventually to come as partner to Alex was something which never entered my head at this time.

The first thing that struck me about Alex was his terrific self-confidence. Nobody had greater faith in the qualities of Alex James than Alex James himself – not even Herbert Chapman, and that is saying something. Alex needed all his self-confidence during his first few months at Highbury, for he was very slow to settle down. Chapman, of course, wanted to cast him in the role of Arsenal schemer, whereas, with Preston, Alex had played a more general type of game, and had acquired quite a reputation as a goal scorer. As everybody knows, he ultimately developed into one of the finest constructive footballers of all time – a triumph for his self-reliance, and Herbert Chapman's foresight.

Alex's confidence was reflected on the field by the constant manner in which he called for the ball. Alex had no illusions about his own ability. He knew full well that, once given the ball, he would be able to make excellent use of it. It must not be imagined that he was conceited, however. He was not.

Alex was an individualist out of the true nineteenth-century mould! Off the field, I mean, not on it. When the Arsenal party stayed in an hotel, while visiting the North of England for an away match, Alex was rarely seen up and about before twelve noon on the day of the game!

No one else had this privilege vouchsafed to him. But we did not begrudge Alex his extended lie-in. After-all, we reasoned, genius cannot be expected always to conform with accepted standards! And besides, Alex was very much awake when the time came for the match.

Many and varied are the stories about him. One will suffice, in this instance. At a certain stage in Alex's Arsenal career, Mr. Chapman decided that Alex, rather off form at the time, needed a change of air. Consequently, he informed him, that he was going to be sent on an ocean voyage, at the club's expense. Alex was delighted. Visions of the *Queen Mary* – the luxury liner of the Atlantic – or some other floating hotel, with dance bands, swimming pools and cinemas swam into his vision.

Shortly after he had received the glad news we find our hero standing on a quayside, accompanied by Tom Whittaker, who has been detailed to see him off. "Which is my ship?" asks Alex.

"That one," says Tom.

Alex looks. He looks again. "What, that dirty little tramp steamer?"

"That's the one," replies Tom.

"Well, whoever thinks I'm going on that," explodes Alex, "is making a big mistake."

"The Boss's orders," Tom chimes in gently.

Alex went.

I fully realise what a great contribution Alex made to my success as an outside-left. It was a pleasure to play beside him. We had a well-nigh perfect understanding. I could follow his moves with ease, although other forward colleagues, so Alex told me, found it very difficult. Alex kept well in towards the middle of the field, thereby giving me plenty of room in which to work. Most of the time, he would be looking for balls somewhere on the other wing, while I had absolute charge of my side of the field, standing about fifteen yards inside from the left touch-line. Then Alex would suddenly fasten on to a loose ball, flash it out to me, and I would make for goal as fast as I possibly could.

This move was varied by Alex's beautifully placed short pass inside the back, designed for me to run on to.

Alex was a past master of switching the play from one side of the field to the other and, in consequence, Joey Hulme received almost as many passes from him as I did. Indeed, his cross-field kick to Joey was amazingly accurate. I have seen him take a goal-kick on the volley, and drop it right at Joey's feet, on the other side of the field.

Alex knew just how long to hold the ball, before parting with it – an attribute denied to the vast majority of footballers, who will either bang it to a colleague before they have sufficiently drawn an opponent, or dribble far too long, until the ball is eventually taken from them. Besides all this, Alex was one of the fastest footballers over ten yards I ever came across. Whether he could have lasted for a hundred is highly problematic. Personally, I doubt it. But it is the short spurts which matter, and Alex was a master of these.

Alex and I, contrary to general opinion, did not see very much of one another off the field. Our understanding was not based on two souls "in perfect communion". Alex was eleven years older than I was, besides, he was a married man. It was natural that we should have our own circle of friends.

I have always felt that Alex was unlucky in life – although this may seem something of a paradox, considering his phenomenal success as a footballer. He was, however, presented with very few opportunities. Born in Bellshill, he was never given the advantages of a really thorough education. Thrown out to fight the world unarmed, he struggled through to the top. A magnificent achievement, but he might, I feel, have made more of the opportunities which consequently accrued to him had such an education been his.

Be that as it may, Alex has left a reputation in Soccer second to none. Whenever the conversation turns, among sport lovers, to great players of the past, his name is always mentioned. And among followers of Arsenal, memories of a shuffling, Puckish little figure, shorts down to his knees and shirt-sleeves flapping loose, will be treasured to the very end.

12
THAT WALSALL AFFAIR

When the draw was made for the Third Round of the F.A. Cup of 1932-33, the red, numbered ball which represented Arsenal came out of the little green bag together with that which denoted Walsall. Walsall were to play at home.

There seemed to be little doubt over the outcome of the game. Arsenal at the time were coasting smoothly along at the head of the First Division, while Walsall were buried deep among the obscure clubs of the Third Division South. Admittedly, the Midland team were the proud possessors of a hundred per cent record at home that season, but the opposition against which this record had been achieved was hardly of the highest calibre. Besides, Walsall had not managed to win away from home that season, and a team which could not even bring off a victory on the ground of a Third Division opponent would hardly seem to have much chance of holding the mighty Arsenal – even if they were playing at home.

Thus reasoned the sporting public of England, when it perused the Third Round draw.

At Highbury, we were all exceptionally keen to make up for last season's heart-breaking defeat in the Cup Final, and it did not seem to us that Walsall were likely to prevent us from breaking through to the Fourth Round. Nevertheless, we were not too happy about our draw.

We never liked to play against Third Division teams. Such teams, when pitted against the glamorous Arsenal, found themselves in a position of having everything to gain and nothing to lose. Consequently, they would fling themselves into the game with reckless abandon and, win, lose, or draw, the gashed, bruised legs of the Arsenal players, after the game was over, would bear grim testimony to their misguided enthusiasm. The Third Division footballer may not be a Soccer artist, but when it comes to a heavy tackle, he ranks with the best.

As was now the Arsenal custom, we went down to Brighton to tune up for the Cup-tie. Whether the opposition was to be Walsall or Aston Villa made no difference to this routine.

At this period, a severe influenza epidemic was sweeping the country, and three of our regular team – Eddie Hapgood, Bob John and Jack Lambert – fell victims to it, shortly before our match was due to be played. Further, Joey Hulme was in the middle of one of those bad periods which come to even the greatest of footballers at one time or another, and, in consequence, Mr. Chapman had some team selection problems on his hands.

In an endeavour to solve them, he chose Tommy Black, who had recently joined Arsenal from a junior Scottish team, to replace Eddie Hapgood. Norman Sidey, our reserve centre-half, took over at left-half, from Bob John; while to take over from Lambert and Joey Hulme, Mr. Chapman chose, respectively, Charlie Walsh and Billy Warnes. In doing so, he made two very rare mistakes.

Warnes, an amateur international, who had come to us from the Isthmian League Club, Woking, was entirely the wrong kind of player for such a match as we were going to play. Essentially an artistic footballer, robust methods were liable to shake him off his game, and he was very chary of involving himself in a full-blooded tackle.

Charlie Walsh had long been trying to bring Chapman round to his way of thinking – that he was the best centre-forward on Arsenal's books – so far, without success. In this match, however, Chapman gave him his chance. He missed it, all too emphatically.

Almost as soon as play had started, on the microscopic Walsall ground, it became quite clear to me that all our fears about the tactics our opponents might employ were fully justified. As soon as the ball came out to me on the left wing I was blatantly fouled by the Walsall right-back, who bowled me over without ceremony. No foul was given, however. Throughout the game, the referee was curiously lenient.

Walsall could not have complained had five of their men, at least, been sent off the field in the first quarter of an hour. Arsenal were awarded ten free-kicks in as many minutes after the first whistle. Compared with this apology for a football match, the replayed Semi-Final against Hull City, three seasons back, had been child's play.

Soon after the kick-off, big Herbie Roberts sustained a cut eye, in a violent aerial collision, and was handicapped accordingly for the rest of the game. Do not misinterpret me. I don't want to level an indictment at the Walsall players. They played, a little too vigorously, perhaps, the game which was right in the circumstances. If David had worn heavy armour against Goliath, the Philistine might have lived to a ripe old age! But it was rather disconcerting for Arsenal.

Yet for all Walsall's crude tactics, and for all the difficulties imposed by the tiny pitch, and the proximity of the spectators who sat around it, I still say we should have won. We had quite enough chances to have banged in half a dozen goals. Not one was accepted.

Charlie Walsh was the chief offender. His nervousness was pitiful to behold. On one occasion, during the first half, I crossed the ball right on to his head, with not one Walsall defender standing within yards of him. His misjudged the centre hopelessly and missed the ball completely. It bounced off his shoulder, to be pounced on by a thankful Walsall defence.

Half-time came without any score. The Walsall supporters cheered their team to the echo, as it came off the field. It had held the mighty Arsenal for fully three-quarters if an hour! How this had been done was a matter that did not need to be discussed.

For the second half, Charlie Walsh was switched to inside-right. David Jack took over from him as centre-forward. Perhaps, we thought, this switch will do the trick. We were wrong.

Walsall took the lead after fifteen minutes. Gilbert Allsop, their centre-forward, headed in a corner taken by the outside-right, Lee. The resultant clamour was heard fully two miles away. This, incidentally, is a fact.

Far from converting the Walsall players to less vigorous ways, this goal only served to encourage them to further excesses of zeal. Alex James, who was literally knocked off his game, was a particularly bad sufferer. The gravest casualty of the second half was, however, left-half Norman Sidey. Norman – a sound player, but always inclined to be a little slow – was moving in leisurely fashion for a ball which he seemed to have plenty of time to bring under control, when a Walsall player appeared on the scene, and kicked him very scientifically on the knee. Sorry as I was for Norman, I must confess that I had to laugh at his resultant antics. He doubled up with pain, then sank slowly, very slowly, to the ground. If he had collapsed at once, it would not have been in the least amusing. But the sight of Norman sinking to the earth in slow motion brought a ray of humour even into this evil-tasting game. Still, isn't it said that humour is always just a step away from tragedy?

If Arsenal had had plenty of chances in the first half, we could not complain of lack of opportunities in the second. On one particular occasion, we would almost certainly have equalised, had it not been for the presence of Charles Walsh.

I gave David Jack a head-high centre. It was a golden chance, and I could sense that David was picking his spot in the Walsall net. But just as the ball was about to reach him, who should come thundering up from behind like a runaway tank but....Charlie Walsh!

The astonishing leap through the air with which he ended his run deserved a better fate than in actually received. Alas, all Charlie did was to divert the ball away from David Jack, far, far from the Walsall goal. I can remember vividly to this day the look which David Jack gave Charlie.

Walsall ultimately made things sure by converting a penalty. It was, I felt, rather curious that we, and not they, should give away a spot-kick, after the manner in which some of their players had behaved. However, there was no doubt at all that the penalty award against us was thoroughly deserved.

It came as the climax of a long series of duels between one of our defenders and a Walsall forward. Relations between these two had gradually been becoming more and more strained, until it ultimately came to a point at which the question was which of them would be the first to vent his feeling on the other. Unfortunately for us, it was our man. The incident was almost followed by a free fight in the Arsenal penalty area, but eventually wisdom prevailed.

Sheppard, the Walsall inside-right, took the penalty. His hard, low shot gave our goalkeeper, Frank Moss, no possible chance of saving.

As soon as the ball was safely in the back of the net, a factory chimney near the ground suddenly began to belch think clouds of black smoke, with the result that the pitch was obscured for several minutes. I felt a little amused at the time. I sensed that the chimney was saying to itself: "Well, we won't let Arsenal score any goals now, anyway!"

Arsenal didn't. The final whistle blew, with the score Walsall 2, Arsenal 0; and, as the frantically happy crowd chaired the Walsall players from the pitch, newspaper correspondents rushed to the telephones to tell the world of Arsenal's sensational defeat.

We certainly were an unhappy team as we changed slowly and moodily in the dressing-room. It was all the more infuriating because we knew we ought to have won. True, the Walsall players had at times behaved more like steamrollers than footballers. True, Charlie Walsh and Billy Warnes had been misfits. Nevertheless, granting all this, we had still been presented with enough chances to have won.

Never have I seen Herbert Chapman look so miserably unhappy. He made a brave, desperate, but unavailing effort to cheer us up. "Never mind, boys," he said, "these things do happen." But we were all inconsolable, and so, for that matter, was he. I think he felt the blow more than any of us. Here was the team which he had come to when it was struggling pathetically at the bottom of the First Division; the team which he had made one of the greatest in the history of football, beaten by a fifth-rate side. Napoleon must have felt like that in Russia, a hundred and twenty-one years before.

Of all the players, I think I felt the effects of the defeat most deeply. At twenty years old, I was the youngest of the side, so perhaps this was only natural. On my way home to my lodgings that night, in the Underground Railway, I felt positively suicidal. Visions of the Arsenal goals that might have been rose up before my eyes; hope that the events of the afternoon had been nothing but an evil nightmare would delude me for a brief moment, only to be banished away by the cold, grim reality.

Walsall 2, Arsenal 0. Nothing could change those figures.

Yet Walsall could hardly be denied some credit for the amazing manner in which they had risen to the occasion. Their tactics, it is true, had been, to say the least of it, somewhat rough and ready, yet it had been obvious that they could not hope to match us with skill, and their only chance lay in putting us off our normal game, by bustling methods. This they had done with astonishing success.

A sequel to this ever-remembered game was the transfer to another club of the man who gave Walsall their penalty. His foul was undoubtedly the result of great provocation, but Mr. Chapman would not suffer behaviour like that from any player at Highbury.

They say that every cloud has a silver lining, and I suppose there were advantages to our Walsall defeat – though nothing would have convinced me of the fact at the time.

The season before we had, of course, fallen between two stools, coming second in the League Championship, and losing to Newcastle in the Cup Final. If we had beaten Walsall, we might easily have done the same again. As it was, we were left to concentrate on the League, and eventually carried it off with several points to spare.

That was certainly some consolation, but the Walsall defeat still rankles in my mind. I believe it always will.

13
ROLL ON, THE GUNNERS!

1931-32 proved merely a temporary set-back. The following season Arsenal cruised to their second League Championship, and then proceeded to equal the record of Huddersfield Town, by winning it the next two seasons, as well. Many were the Arsenal triumphs, and many were the Arsenal goals. I myself enjoyed a great deal of success, winning three League Championship medals, and consolidating my position in the England team.

We scored no less than three hundred and eight goals in those three League Championships, including seven in a game which I shall always remember. That was played on Guy Fawkes' Day, 1932, when Arsenal provided the fireworks at the Molineux Ground, Wolverhampton.

So far, in that 1932-33 season, Arsenal had been unbeaten away from home. As we had also scored nineteen goals in our last four games, and were sitting on top of the League, it was no easy task that faced Wolves. Any forebodings they may have had were fully justified. The match stands out in my memory as one of the finest Arsenal have ever played. It seemed that nothing could go wrong. Seven times did the Wolverhampton goalkeeper pick the ball out of the net; and only once were the Buckley Boys able to reply. The game was made especially interesting for me by the fact that my opponent at right-back was Wilf Lowton, who, of course, had captained Exeter City when I played my first games in professional football. Perhaps it was rather unfair of me, but I had one of my best days against Wilf, and scored two of our seven goals. He himself contributed to my success, however, by the curious tactics he adopted. Instead of marking me closely on the wing, Wilf spent most of the game standing in his own goal mouth. Consequently, I had yards of room in which to move, and ample time to put across my centres. Poor Rhodes, the Wolves right-half, was virtually left with both Alex James and myself to mark. But however Wilf had played, I think he will admit that nothing could have stopped us that afternoon. We were going through the Wolverhampton defence without any of their players touching the ball.

That season, we won the League with fifty-eight points: not, of course, to be compared with our sixty-six points effort of two seasons ago, but nevertheless, apart from our own record, the highest Championship points achieved since 1924-25. In the Cup, 1933 saw us make an inglorious exit in the Third Round, in a match of which I have had something to say in a previous chapter.

For my own part, that season was one of the finest I have ever enjoyed. I did not regain the England place which I had lost after my international debut before the close-season Continental tour – of which more later – but I set up a record of goals from the wing which has not yet been equalled by any Football League player, under the new offside-rule. I played forty-two games, all of them at outside-left and found the net on thirty-three occasions. Like most records set up at Arsenal, however, mine was not marked by undue feasting and revelry.

The following campaign we retained the Championship, with fifty-nine points to Huddersfield Town's fifty-six. I scored fourteen goals, twenty fewer than the previous season, but I am reminded of this season not by these goals, but rather by two representative games in which I took part. Before I go on to discuss these, I may as well remark, in parenthesis, that the F.A. Cup again eluded us, although this time we managed to get as far as the Sixth Round. We won away at Luton in our first match, 1-0, thanks to a goal headed by our centre-forward, Jimmy Dunne. That season, Jimmy had joined us from Sheffield United, to replace Jack Lambert, who departed for Fulham. Jimmy, a big, fair-headed Irishman, with a curious, short-stepping run, had been a great player in his day. As I have already mentioned earlier on, Herbert Chapman had long been keen to sign him. But when he at last succeeded, it was too late. Jimmy was past his best. However, his goal was the means of giving us victory that day.

We went on to beat Crystal Palace 7-0 and Derby County 1-0 at Highbury, but the Villa put us out at home in the next round, by the odd goal in three. However, to return to the subject of these two representative games.

The first of these was against the Irish League, at Preston. I was picked as inside-left to Manchester City's Eric Brook, which pleased me greatly. I always felt that inside-left was my best position, and, somehow or other, was quite confident that I would have a good match. So it transpired. The whole Football League team, in fact, had a successful day, but it must be confessed that the opposition provided by the Irish team was of a very low standard. Seldom, in fact, have I played in an easier game; seldom has everything gone my way as it did that afternoon.

Eric Brook and I interchanged at will – as, indeed, we always did, when partnering one another – and it was from one of our switches that the first goal resulted. Eric ran inside, I put the ball through to him, he sent Derby's Sammy Crooks away on the right wing, and from Sammy's centre, Jack Bowers headed into the net. I scored from a penalty-kick before half-time, and in the second period we scored two more, to make the final tally, Football League 4, Irish League 0. The score, however, was purely incidental. We might have reached double figures.

Not an important or even outstanding match in itself, but for me it was one of the happiest ever. There had been a lot of talk around at the time of finding an adequate inside-left for England, and, the following day, one of the sports writers paid me the compliment of saying that mine was the finest exhibition of inside-left play that he had seen in twenty years. The England selectors were evidently satisfied, for they picked me to play at inside-left in the full International against Ireland, immediately after the Inter-League game was over.

Unlike this Inter-League affair, the other game in season 1933-34 which will, I think, be always fresh in my memory was one which was significant in itself – England v Scotland, at Wembley. I had a great thrill when I learned that I had been chosen – again at inside-left. It was my first ever game against Scotland, and this my first International at Wembley, although, of course, I had already appeared there twice in Cup Finals.

The full England team was to be as follows:

Moss (Arsenal); Cooper (Derby County); Hapgood (Arsenal); Stoker (Birmingham); Hart (Leeds United); Copping (Leeds United); Crooks (Derby County); Carter (Sunderland); Bowers (Derby County); myself; Brook (Manchester City).

It certainly looked a strong team on paper, and I felt that, even if we failed to beat the Scots, we should at least give them a very hard fight. They had already lost both their previous International matches that season, while we had beaten Ireland, and lost to Wales. The previous year, the Hampden roar had urged the Scots on to a 2-1 victory, but the April before that they had bitten the Wembley dust to the tune of 3-0. I hoped for a repeat performance, against a formidable-looking side:

Jackson (Chelsea); Anderson (Hearts); McGonagle (Celtic); Massie (Hearts); Smith (Kilmarnock); Miller (St. Mirren); Cook (Bolton); Marshall (Rangers); Gallagher (Chelsea); Stevenson (Motherwell); Connor (Sunderland).

It was a great game to play in; cut-and-thrust by both sides, in the tense, roaring atmosphere which characterises clashes between the two countries. I had a special incentive to do well, for it was the first, in fact only, time that my father watched me play in an International. It was good to know that he was in the stand. It was good too, to have my Arsenal colleagues, Eddie Hapgood and Frank Moss, playing with me. They, also, were taking part in their first games against the blue-shirted Scots.

I certainly had my shooting boots on, I thought, as Johnny Jackson pushed a drive from me over the bar, and then punched out another. It was England all the way for the first quarter of an hour, and when at last we scored, I don't think the goal could have been begrudged us: not even by the tartan-bonneted dervishes, capering wilding on the Wembley terraces.

The goal game from a left-wing movement. Wilf Copping, later to become a colleague of mine at Highbury, started an England attack. From one man to another went the ball, until, suddenly, fair-headed Eric Brook had it, out on the left touch-line. Down the wing tore Eric, with the blue-shirted Scottish defenders hard upon his heels. Before they could catch up with him, however, he had turned the ball back to me. It was a beautiful pass; running just how I wanted it. I ran on to the ball, and hit it first time with my left foot. Johnny Jackson dived; touched it, but it whizzed under his body, and into the Scottish net. We were one up.

We kept that lead until half-time. During the interval, however, something came over that Scottish team. They took on a new lease of life, and subjected our defence to a terrific hammering. Frank Moss leaped from one side of his goal to the other, dealing with shot after shot, while Eddie Hapgood, cool and polished as ever, even during this Scottish bombardment, stood firm with the rest of the English rearguard against all attacks.

As is so often the case, however, it was a breakaway that decided.

The ball was cleared out to me, and I went racing away down field at top speed. I had all but reached the edge of the Scottish penalty area when somebody crashed against me in an unceremonious last-ditch tackle, and I fell heavily to the ground. In spite of the Scottish protests, the referee awarded a foul. Eric Brook, one of the most powerful kickers of a dead ball football has ever known, took the free-kick. A terrific shot against the solid blue wall of Scottish defenders; a desperate lunge by right-back Anderson, a ricochet, and...the ball was in the net again! England 2, Scotland 0.

Alec Massie, the Scottish captain, and other members of his team, declared vigorously after the game that I had not been fouled. Perhaps things may have appeared differently to them, but I was on the receiving end of that tackle, and I can assure them that fouled I certainly was. The altogether curious nature of this goal took the fight out of Scotland, and Jack Bowers headed a third goal for England.

The final score, then, was, England 3, Scotland 0; although at one period of the game such a clear-cut victory for us had appeared most unlikely, to say the least of it. That grand match was memorable to me for several reasons. For one thing, it was the only time I ever scored a goal at Wembley, although I was destined to play there on four further occasions. Incidentally, I learned after the game that my scoring shot had nearly broken poor Johnny Jackson's fingers! Another interesting feature of the match, so far as I was concerned, was that it was the only time I played on the winning side against Scotland.

Before it, several sports writers had expressed doubts as to whether I would make the grade as England's inside-left. After the game was over, they glibly covered up their mistakes. This was something which always used to annoy me intensely, about sports writers. Many of them were, and for that matter still are, essentially sensationalists. Often, a startling forecast or story was printed which subsequently turned out to be an utter false piece of prophecy. But the writer in question went gaily on his way. Seldom indeed did one do public penance for his error, although he was always ready to indict a player on one indifferent game. Still, I myself am now a writer on the staff of the *Sunday Pictorial*, and find it easier to see the sporting journalist's point of view!

England 3, Scotland 0. A fine victory, and a tonic which I badly needed. For three months previously I had received a terrible, staggering blow, whose memory, haunting and bitter, remains with me, even to this day.

14
THE CHANGING SCENE AT HIGHBURY

January 6th, 1934. The telephone bell rang in my London home. I picked up the receiver. It was my friend, Ralph Reader. His voice sounded strained and taut. "I'm afraid I've got some very bad news for you, Cliff. Herbert Chapman is dead."

The news came to me as a terrible shock. I could not have felt it more had it been the death of my own father. As if things were not bad enough, the day was a Saturday, and Arsenal were due to play a match at Highbury, against Sheffield Wednesday. As I approached the ground, that afternoon, the placards of the newspaper-sellers were shouting out the news of Chapman's death. It seemed just too bad to be true. In the Arsenal dressing-room, nobody had anything to say, yet each of us knew what his companions were thinking. Herbert Chapman had been loved by all of us. His fairness, his kind-heartedness, his consideration, above all else, for the players under his charge, were qualities which, besides his transcendent genius, ensured a cherished place for him in the memories if all who had come under his magic spell, at Highbury.

Both teams stood to attention before the kick-off, in memory of the man who had died that morning. I suppose Arsenal gave quite a good display that day, considering that, to every one of the players, the game was just an unimportant incident, and Chapman's death a terrible reality. Even the crowd was practically silent, throughout the ninety minutes of a game which, to me, seemed to go on for ninety years.

I managed to keep my feelings in check until after the funeral. Then, coming out of the church, I broke down completely. Herbie Roberts, who felt the loss as much as I did, held himself in check, and did his best to comfort me.

But it was Tom Whittaker who was more affected than any of us. At the end of the funeral service, he was wandering about in the road outside the church, dazed by grief. It was a wonder that he escaped being run down by a car. Tom told me later that, for several mornings after Chapman's death, he heard the chiming clock in his room strike 3 a.m., though he never heard it chime at any other hour. It was at 3 a.m. that Chapman had died.

The natural successor to Herbert Chapman was our assistant manager, Joe Shaw; a man who had worshipped Chapman, who was well versed in all his methods, and had the complete confidence of all the Arsenal players. Joe, alas, preferred to be the man behind the scenes, rather than to be focused in the blinding glare of publicity which would inevitably surround the new Arsenal manager.

The man who did take over the position was one to whom the limelight was far from unwelcome: Mr. George F. Allison, a member of the Arsenal board of directors. Mr. Allison was a prominent journalist, closely connected with the powerful concern of Hearst's Newspapers, and a man with a natural flare for publicity. He was not, however, a successor shaped in the Chapman mould. Indeed, relations between him and Mr. Chapman had not always been of the happiest. With consummate ease, he had the name of Arsenal splashed across the front pages of the British Press, but he lacked Herbert Chapman's gift of getting the best out of his players.

It is said that, just before he died, Herbert Chapman had told his successor: "The team's played out, Mr. Allison. We must rebuild." At all events, new faces soon began to appear at Highbury, and well before the end of 1934 it was a new-look Arsenal team which played before its supporters at Highbury. And Highbury, too, had changed, for in 1932 the magnificent new West Stand had been declared open by His Royal Highness the Prince of Wales. We had celebrated the occasion by defeating Chelsea in a League match.

Already, George Male had taken the place of Tom Parker at right-back, and was shaping to become an even better player than the man he had replaced. Now, at wing-half, the stalwart all-Welsh partnership of Charlie Jones and Bob John was broken up, and two Yorkshiremen took its place. Like their predecessors, these two were utter contrasts in character, and far greater contrasts in style. Yet they were the greatest friends, and were almost inseparable off the field of play. Their names? Jack Crayston and Wilf Copping.

Jack came to us from Bradford, to take the place of Charlie Jones. Smartly dressed, debonair and a total abstainer, this grand, likeable fellow always prided himself on being in bed before ten o'clock at night. Jack had splendid physique, which helped him to become one of the longest throw-in experts the game has ever known, fine ball control, and was unrivalled in the air by any wing-half I have seen. Another feature of his play was the way he cut through an opposing defence at speed. Destined to become an English International, Jack was every bit as good as Charlie Jones: which is paying him a great compliment. In fact, if I had to give a decision between the two of them, perhaps I would award it to Jack, by the narrowest of hairbreadths. Jack, of course, is now assistant manager of Arsenal.

Wilf Copping, his partner at wing-half, came to us at an £8,000 fee from Leeds United. I had already had this tough, dark, hard-tackling footballer playing behind me in international matches. Wilf was the Wallace Beery of football. Hard as nails and with the heart of a lion, he never knew when he was beaten. But he was lacking in the arts of the game, and although he was a good man to have on your side, he did not have the polish of Jack Crayston, or of Bob John, who had gone before him.

At inside-forward the Jack-James era ended, and a new partner arrived at Highbury for Alex. He was Raymond Bowden, who came to us from Plymouth. He was the natural successor to David. Like him, he was a stylist, and he possessed the very same elusive swerve which had made David such a menace to opposing defences. In fact, he had everything that a footballer should have – except the right temperament. Ray was capable of being a great player on some days. On others, he was very disappointing. He gained several caps for England, whilst he was at Highbury, yet I feel that he never really settled down with us. Injuries to his ankles played a part in this. Eventually, Ray was transferred to Newcastle United. He did not want to go. Indeed, he had not been over-anxious to travel as far north from Plymouth, where he had a sports outfitter's shop, as London. He found the atmosphere at Newcastle congenial to him, however – he and Mr. Allison had not always been the best of friends, at Highbury – and told me afterwards that he thought Newcastle a fine club, which treated its players well. Judging by the phenomenal transfer activity which had centred around Newcastle, since the recent war, the same happy atmosphere as prevailed then is not quite so much in evidence, now.

Another inside-right who came to us during this period was Dr. James Marshall, from Glasgow Rangers. The Doctor, a Scottish International, had first attracted the attention of Arsenal with a terrific first-time goal he had scored against us at Highbury for the Rangers, in 1933. Mysteriously, he never revealed any glimpse of that form at Highbury. Very much addicted to day-dreaming, Marshall's style was far too slow to fit in with the Arsenal scheme of things. "What's the matter with you, Doc?" Joey Hulme would ask. "Somebody treading on your laces?" The Doctor, who went into partnership with Dr. Pepper, the club's medical consultant, left us after a short period for West Ham, but even at Upton Park he failed to show the form which had brought him caps for Scotland.

One other man gained for himself a regular place in the Arsenal team, and that was Ted Drake. Ever since Lambert had left us, the centre-forward position had been a problem to Highbury. Ted, who joined us from Southampton, solved it. Ted was the type of centre-forward Arsenal required: a dashing, fearless player, who would go through for goal at the slimmest opportunity. He had terrific speed, great strength, and an immensely powerful shot. A nightmare to any centre-half, he was particularly good on turning to advantage the long ball, punted down the middle.

Yet although Ted gained five caps for England – and might have had more, were it not for the persistent injuries which followed naturally upon his impetuous style – I did not consider him as good a centre-forward as Jack Lambert. Jack was more of a footballer, and his style of play fitted in much better with my own than did Ted's. Jack did a good deal of wandering, out on the wings. Ted, on the other hand, took the centre of the field as his lawful preserve. When he received the ball, he would charge straight down the middle, taking it, and often the attendant centre-half, with him. And whenever the ball centred near goal Ted considered it his duty to put it into the net. Very often, he did. Often too, however, he would take it virtually off my foot, as I was about to shoot.

In season 1934-35, his first full season with Arsenal, Ted scored forty-two League goals: a magnificent performance, and one which stands as an Arsenal record. Ted has always been a very lively fellow, and what with both Joey Hulme and him in the team, there were few dull moments. Typical of the tricks he would play was one he perpetrated on Bobby Davidson, inside-right, who came to us early in 1935, from St. Johnstone. Bobby, a lively and rather fiery little fellow, prided himself on his knowledge and correct observance of Sassenach customs. Alas for him, he shared lodgings with Ted! One day, the two of them were sitting together at lunch, listening to the radio, when suddenly the programme which they were hearing came to an end, and the band played *God Save the King*. Ted at once dropped his knife and fork, and sprang out of his chair to rigid attention. Bobby looked up at him with a puzzled frown, and then immediately followed suit. The band went right through the National Anthem, and there were Bobby and Ted standing all through it, as if they were taking part in the Changing of the Guard! Ted managed to contain himself until the band had finished playing. Then he went into a fit of uncontrollable laughter. Little Bobby suddenly realised the joke that had been played on him, and for the next few minutes he proceeded to turn the air blue!

Ted gained his first England cap in an International match in which, I think, I had one of the best games of my career – against Ireland, at Goodison Park, the Everton ground. Besides Ted and myself, there were three other Arsenal men in the England side that day. Eddie Hapgood, partnered by George Male, was left-back and captain, while Wilf Copping was behind me, at left-half. Eric Brook was once again my outside-left, while the game Irish team included Peter Doherty, then with Blackpool, Wolverhampton's "Boy" Martin, a namesake of mine, and Everton's speedy outside-left, Jackie Coulter. The Irishmen gave us a hard fight, but we managed to squeeze home by the odd goal of three – and I scored twice.

Five men in an England team from one club was an excellent achievement, but it did not bear comparison with Arsenal's effort in another match that season, against Italy, in November 1934. To start with, five Arsenal players were chosen for the match, which was to take place at Highbury: Frank Moss; Eddie Hapgood; Wilf Copping; Ray Bowden; and myself. This was my second game against Italy, for I had already played against them in 1933, in a match of which I shall have more to say later. Then, however, I had been at outside-left, whereas now I was chosen in the inside position. The Arsenal membership had swelled to six, when George Male was brought in to replace the injured Tom Cooper: his first international selection. Finally, Freddy Tilson, the selected centre-forward, was injured. Tottenham's George Hunt was invited to fill the breach, but the gods were smiling on Arsenal. George had to decline the invitation, through injury, and Ted Drake, like George Male, was honoured with his first cap. Just to make everything perfect, Tom Whittaker was appointed trainer to the side, and Eddie Hapgood was made captain!

The four non-Arsenal members of the side were Cliff Britton, of Everton, at right-half, Derby County's hefty Jack Barker, in the centre-half position, and Stanley Matthews (Stoke) and Eric Brook (Manchester City) on the wings. The Italian team at that time was one of the finest in the world. They had won the World Cup earlier in the year, a competition in which the British teams had not been competing, and I knew that they would give us a very hard game. More was the pity, then, that Mussolini had offered them such terrific incentives if they beat us that their play deteriorated, in their over-eagerness, to a patchwork series of clever moves and questionable tactics. This was their team:

Ceresoli (Internazionale); Monzeglio (Bologna); Allemandi (Internazionale); Ferraris (Lazio) Monti (Juventus); Bertolini (Juventus); Guaita (Roma); Serrantoni (Juventus); Meazza (Internazionale) ; Ferrari (Juventus) ; Orsi (Juventus).

For the first twenty minutes of the game we outplayed them. Ceresoli, their brilliant goalkeeper, saved a penalty from Eric Brook, but Eric was not worried by his first minute miss, and proceeded to atone for it with two fine goals. England were playing brilliant football, and the Italians became a little riled. Ferraris, their right-half, deliberately elbowed Eddie Hapgood in the face, breaking his nose, but, while Eddie was off the field, Ted Drake slammed home a third, and we were all set for victory.

The Italians, however, were no mean opponents. Like several of the Continental countries I played against, they were remarkably fit and tough, and when I came into a tackle with one of them, I felt as if I had come up against a brick wall. They were splendidly led my Meazza, their centre-forward, and the idol of Italy, who gave Frank Moss a most hectic afternoon. Eddie Hapgood's was not the only injury, for the Italian skipper and centre-half, Monti, injured his foot, and had to leave the field.

There was no denying that the Italians did resort to unfair tactics, after they were a couple of goals down, but, nevertheless, I think that reports of this game have been greatly exaggerated. The newspaper reporter is almost always on the look-out for a sensational story, and this match provided him with an ideal opportunity to show his skill. I myself have played in many far "dirtier" games, and the match in Zurich against Switzerland, in 1939, was an infinitely more unscrupulous one, so far as our opponents were concerned, than was this.

Meazza scored two quick goals for Italy, in the second half, but Frank Moss flung himself all over his goal, to prevent them finding the net again. From the playing point of view, I have no outstanding recollection of this game, although Eddie Hapgood, in his *Football Ambassador*, writes that I played like a hero, so I suppose that I must have done quite well. My chief memory of this match, however, is a letter which I received after it, from a woman who had attended the game, in which she told me how much she had appreciated the sportsmanship I displayed. Never before or since have I had a letter like it, although letters of congratulation – and abuse! – on my actual play have been frequent. I was deeply touched by it.

Perhaps the greatest success of the match was Wilf Copping. It certainly was a day for the tough player, rather than the artist, and Wilf revelled in the conditions. The following day, Jack Crayston, who had watched the game, walked into Mr. Allison's office and said: "If we play Italy tomorrow, there's only one half-back line to put out!"

"What's that?" asked Mr. Allison.

"Copping, Copping and Copping!" was Jack's reply.

15
ABROAD WITH ENGLAND

"Don't ever go to London, Cliff!" grandmother had said. But if I hadn't gone to London, I would never have joined Arsenal; if I hadn't joined Arsenal, I would never have played for England, and if I had never played for England, I would not have been afforded a Continental holiday at the Football Association's expense, at the tender age of twenty-one. All this is just to say that I was chosen by the English selectors to go on the European tour of 1933.

It came to me as a very pleasant surprise when I was selected, not only because of the visit to Italy and Switzerland which it meant, but because I had not gained any International caps that season, and did not even have a Football League cap to show for my endeavours. With me was to go Eddie Hapgood, who thus received his first International recognition: the start of a long and distinguished England career. Another companion was to be no less a person than Mr. Herbert Chapman, who was travelling unofficially with the England party; a great comfort to me, on only the second occasion I had left England, except to play football in Scotland! My first tour had been with Arsenal in Scandinavia, three years earlier.

Our first match was to be in Rome, against Italy. Never before had England met Italy in an International, and reports had it that the Italians were frantically keen to win. We knew that no easy game awaited us, for two years previously Scotland had gone down by three clear goals, in the cradle of civilisation. Besides, English football prestige was slipping. The Austrians had come within an ace of beating us at Stamford Bridge, and the 4-3 win which we had gained had really been more than we had deserved. Defeat by Italy would be a crushing blow. Certainly, the Italians were leaving no stone unturned, in their preparations to beat us – if they could. They had imported Herr Hugo Meisl, the Herbert Chapman of Austria, the man behind the Austrian display at Chelsea, to coach their team. "Watch Bastin!" he had advised the Italian defence. I felt highly complimented, but a little apprehensive about the amount of scope I would be allowed.

I was idolised from the very moment I stepped off the train in Rome. I don't know what Reuter and Herr Meisl had been telling them, but the Italians seemed to be under the impression that I was going to play their International team on my own!

It was a wonderful experience, visiting Rome. We saw the mighty St. Peter's, with its wonderful sculptures by Michelangelo, its magnificent chapel by Benvenuto Cellini; the Roman Forum, almost the same then, but for the macadamised roads and the motor traffic, as it had been, thousands of years ago. We visited the Colosseum, in whose bowl the early Christians were once thrown to the wild beasts, and which now is filled by the ruined masonry built there only recently – in the eleventh century, to be exact! We saw, too, the ruins of Pompei, and the Capitol Hill, where the geese once shrieked to the city that the Gauls would soon be at its gates.

But what left the greatest impression on my mind was the regimentation of the city. Everybody seemed to be in uniform: policemen, postmen, nurses, taxi-drivers: even the very street-cleaners wore some distinctive attire. It was my first experience of the Fascist State.

Just before the International Match was due, Mr. Chapman was put in charge of the team. It was a great and well-merited honour for him. Never before or since has the manager of a professional club held such a position, although Tom Whittaker, when assistant manager of Arsenal, was appointed England team manager for the match against France, in 1946.

It was while sitting with Mr. Chapman at a garden-party given in the England team's honour that I was besieged by two Italians, who bombarded me in their own tongue. Since I was not conversant with it, they were merely wasting their own time and mine, but an interpreter explained to me that they were newspaper reporters, and wanted to know how many goals I was going to score in the match, the following day. "Tell them five," I said, light-heartedly. The next morning, glaring headlines proclaimed that I was going to score five times against Italy – after all, had I not said so?

The England line-up for the game was as follows: Hibbs (Birmingham); Goodall (Huddersfield Town); Hapgood (Arsenal); Strange (Sheffield Wednesday); White (Everton); Copping (Leeds United); Geldard (Everton); Richardson (Newcastle United); Hunt (Tottenham); Furness (Leeds United), myself.

The Italian team was: Combri; Rosetta (holder of forty-four caps); Calligaris; Rizziolo; Monti; Bertolini; Constantino; Meazza; Schiavio; Ferraria; Orsi.

It was a hot day and a small ground, neither of which conditions was particularly helpful to England. The Italians shook us, by scoring in four minutes. Harry Hibbs, always a nervous starter, slipped in the act of saving a shot from inside-left Ferraria, and the ball flashed into the net. Harry was most upset.

I myself was being closely policed by the Italian defenders, who were not always too restrained in their methods, but I was managing to give them the slip quite often. After twenty-three minutes play I scored our equaliser. I collected a long pass from the right, beat my right-half, whose job it was, under Italian tactics, to mark me, while the back kept inside, and cut in for goal. His hand clutched desperately at my shirt, but he luckily failed to grasp it. I waited until the right moment had arrived, then beat Combri with a left-foot drive, into the corner of the net. Harry Hibbs, thankful that his mistake had been nullified, ran the whole length of the field to congratulate me.

At half-time, there was momentary panic in the England camp, when Herbert Chapman could not recover the key to the dressing-room which he had so carefully locked up. Concerned as ever about the welfare of the players, Mr. Chapman rushed here, there and everywhere, growing more hot and worried, until at last the wretched key was found, and we were able to get into our dressing-room.

The second half yielded no more goals, but was made memorable for me by the spectators' constant cry of "Basta Bastin! Basta Bastin!" which, not being so rude as it may sound, means "Enough of Bastin!" Curiously, perhaps, it was the Italians who adopted the traditional British long-passing game, while we advanced with short passes. It was a match which I enjoyed, and as I walked off the field, with the ball under my arm, the crowd of 50,000 Italians gave me an ovation.

We stayed in Rome for a few days after the game, and had audiences with the Pope and Mussolini. I shall always remember both of them – but particularly the latter. We were ushered into the beautiful palace where the Dictator lived – a palace which, ironically, was dedicated to peace. Mussolini had evidently decided to keep us waiting. At last his bodyguards came into the room, and, eventually, the Dictator himself entered, resplendent in morning dress. Never have I known such an astonishing personality. I have always considered Herbert Chapman to have been outstanding in this respect, but compared with Mussolini on this occasion he was an utter nonentity. Yet the man did nothing. Nothing whatsoever. Perhaps it was merely the clever way in which he had kept us in suspense that produced the effect it did, but suffice it that is was an effect which I, for one, shall never forget: and I don't think any member of the England party who was present will, either.

From Italy we went on to Switzerland: but not before I had been deluded into buying my dearest drink ever! This happened when we visited a cafe in Rome, one evening. The proprietor was delighted to see us. Could he announce that we were here, he asked? Drinks, of course, would be on the house. He could announce it if he liked, we told him. So the loudspeakers in the cafe blared out the news that the England party was present, and we all stood up on our chairs, and felt rather self-conscious.

Since drinks were on the house, I decided it would do no harm to have a beer – although I very seldom drank. Then, after about half an hour in the cafe, we returned to our hotel. All well and good. The following morning, however, we were greeted by the news that the bill for our drinks had arrived! This in itself was something of a surprise, but when we saw the price which had been charged us, some of us nearly fell over backwards! For my own part, my beer had cost me five shillings and four-pence! Angry though we were, we decided to pay the bill; and be more careful in the future. So much for drinks on the house. I wonder what my beer would have cost had I paid for it at the normal, unsubsidised rate?

The game against Switzerland, like that against Italy the first between the two countries, was to take place in Berne, but we stayed at Interlaken. I was fascinated by the picturesque Swiss scenery; the great mountains, with their peaks of never-melting snow; the rushing icy torrents; the cows with the jangling bells hung around their necks. We went up the Jungfrau and several lesser mountains by funicular, and feasted our eyes on the icy splendour of the Rhone glacier.

Our team for the match showed two changes from the one which had drawn with Italy: O'Dowd, of Chelsea, replaced White at centre-half, Eric Brook was to play at outside-left, while I moved to the inside position, to the exclusion of Furness.

Although Eric and I were rivals for the England outside-left position – the selectors usually compromised by putting me at inside-left and Eric on the wing – we were always the greatest of friends. Eric was invariably the life and soul of the party, on tours. A comedian, pianist and singer, he could always be relied on to lighten the dull moments. Another accomplished entertainer was centre-forward George Hunt, who later came to Highbury. Gay, debonair George was a really accomplished pianist, in the Charlie Kunz rhythm style.

Eric Brook, to return to my original subject, was a strong, direct, dangerous player, whose purposeful roaming and terrific left-foot made him a menace to defenders, although he could not lay much claim to football artistry.

The Swiss put up a gallant performance, but we won easily enough, in this game at the Neufield Stadium. I put us ahead in the first half, and we scored three more without reply in the second: another from me, and two from Newcastle's Richardson. Let Reuter have the last word on this game and, indeed, the whole tour: *"Bastin bewildered the Swiss defence. After his brilliant performance against Italy, he has earned for himself a name second to none on the Continent. Whether at inside-left as in the first-half, or on the wing as in the second, he was equally versatile, and was the prime mover in a speedy attack."* I said, let Reuter have the last word, but I cannot resist making a correction to this statement. Although every newspaper said so, Eric Brook and I never changed places, in the second half. I think it was our frequent interchanging of positions which led the newspaper reporters into believing that we had. So much for the England tour of 1933.

The following year, I was again selected for the England party. This time, however, we were destined to be by no means so successful. In fact, our Balkan tour resulted in two odd goal defeats. There were too many players slow in recovery included in our team; men who would just stand still, after they had been beaten in a tackle, instead of running back to challenge, as they should.

Eddie Hapgood was again included in the England party, and so, too, was Frank Moss: a fitting reward for his magnificent display against Scotland, the previous April. Our first destination was Budapest, where we were to meet Hungary. I found the city one of the most beautiful that I have ever seen. The Hungarians call it "Queen of the Danube", and at this time, before Budapest had been scarred by opposing armies, it was easy to understand their proud boast. I found it a city of beautiful panoramas; of quaint cobbled streets intermingled with majestic boulevards; of wide squares, lined with imposing buildings, and dotted with monuments, and unexpected gardens. Above all, I felt the city was alive. Everybody seemed to be happy, and at night-time the Hungarians lived their bright, gay life in the wayside cafes. Today, I understand that the picture is sadly different: every one of the seven bridges linking the towns of Buda and Pest was blown up by the Germans during the recent war, and I don't suppose a traveller would find the same spontaneous gaiety there. But in 1934 Budapest was worth visiting.

Our hotel was situated on its most popular promenade, and never have I seen so many pretty girls and smartly dressed men as I did then. As usual, we were shown the sites; among them, a swimming bath with artificial waves, an innovation which was adopted in later years at the Empire Pool, Wembley.

It was a baking hot day when we met the dashing Hungarians. They proved themselves one of the finest sides I have ever played against. We did not have a good team, and it was only the brilliance of Frank Moss, in goal, which saved us from a heavier beating than we actually sustained. The positional play of the Hungarians was first-class, and had their finishing not been so poor, even Frank could not have stopped them scoring five or six goals – as they deserved to. They attacked from the start, but it took twenty minutes before Avar, their inside-right, opened the scoring. Five minutes later, centre-forward Sarosi added a second. Freddy Tilson, our centre-forward, scored a consolation goal for us, six minutes from time, after a goal-mouth scramble.

As always, the England party was a lively one on this tour, and one of the features of it was an excursion into bookmaking by Sammy Crooks, Derby County's outside-right. He blithely announced that he was prepared to accept bets on the Derby, which had been run some days previously. As English newspapers took some time to arrive in the Balkans, however, the results were not yet known to us. When they ultimately did come, poor Sammy wished they hadn't! It had been a backer's day, and he had to pay out quite a lot of money!

Another amusing incident occurred when we bought an English newspaper containing an article which advocated that British sportsmen should be given titles. Among the names mentioned was my own, and for the rest of the tour I was addressed by all as Count Cliff!

On to Prague, where Czechoslovakia were to be met. I did not find this city anything like as intriguing as Budapest. The people were unfriendly and sullen, and I missed the spontaneous good-fellowship which the Hungarians had displayed.

We changed in our hotel before the game, and went from there straight to the pitch. There was no dressing-room accommodation. The pitch itself might have had one or two blades of grass on it. If it did, I failed to notice them. The Hungarian ground had been bad enough, but this one had been heavily watered for two whole days before, and had been baked hard as a rock by the scorching heat of the sun. Besides this, it had been trampled by hundreds of people, just before the game.

We lost again that day, although we scored the first goal. This came after twenty minutes. Sammy Crooks, out in the right wing, beat his man, and Freddy Tilson headed us into the lead from Sammy's beautifully placed centre.

The Czechs, however, were a fine team, almost as good as the Hungarians, and they wiped out their arrears four minutes from half-time, when Nekedly, their inside-left, ran between our backs, and beat Frank Moss with a terrific drive. This goal was largely due to the fact that Ernie Hart, an attacking centre-half, was caught somewhere around the neighbourhood of the half-way line, and had been unable to recover in time.

Puc, the Czech centre-forward, won the game for his team, shortly after half-time, but his goal was yards offside. Wally Lewington, the linesman whom we had brought with us, waved his flag vigorously, but to no avail. The referee ignored him completely. We were not helped, either, by a knee injury to our left-half, Gardner, who was hobbling for most of the second half.

Once again, it was Frank Moss who saved us from a greater defeat. I have always maintained that he showed his true greatness on this tour. He was beaten altogether four times, when any ordinary goalkeeper would have conceded a dozen or more goals. Alas, the following year Frank was destined to receive the shoulder injury which prevented him from becoming the finest goalkeeper of all time.

Presentation at Exeter.

Bastin scores against Italy, Rome, 1933.

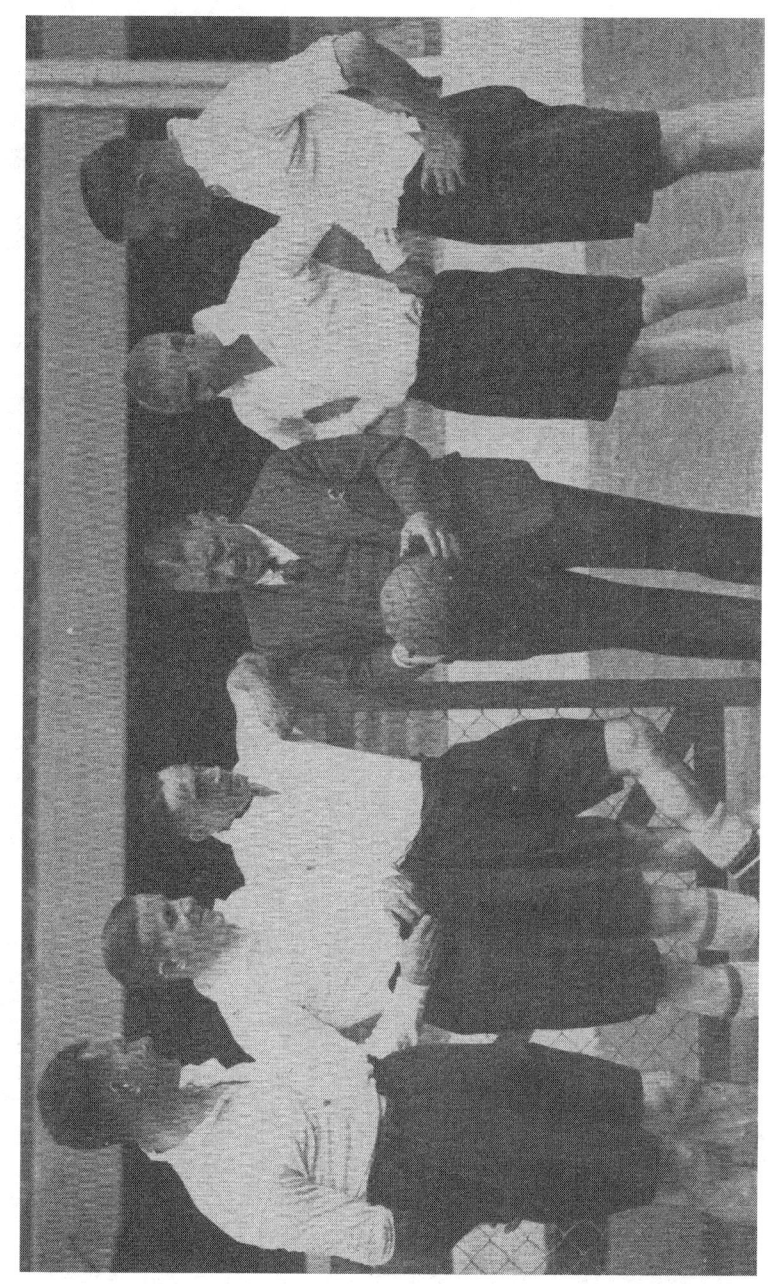

George Allison takes over at Highbury.

Six Arsenal internationals.

Bastin in action, England *versus* Scotland, Wembley, 1938.

Bastin in play *versus* Everton, 1938.

Arsenal *versus* Sunderland at Highbury, Bastin scoring for Arsenal, 1939.

Arsenal team, 1939.

16

WE WIN THE CUP AGAIN

For six long years the Cup had eluded Arsenal. Always, when the time for the season's Cup-ties came round, we hoped for the best, and played our hardest. In 1932, we had come within an ace of bringing the Cup to Highbury once more, but since then we had not been able to get any further than the Sixth Round. In the 1935 tournament we had been cursed with four away draws in a row. We had defeated Brighton, Leicester and Reading, without conceding a goal, but Sheffield Wednesday, the eventual Cup winners, had squeezed us out 2-1, at Hillsborough.

Now, in 1936, we were drawn away in our first match to Bristol Rovers. We were not particularly pleased. Memories of that Walsall affair were still fresh, while, as I have said before, we at Arsenal never did like being drawn against Third Division teams. The first half of the match justified our fears. The Rovers' bustling tactics put us off our game, and Houghton, their ex-Everton inside-left, and a very clever ball player, gave them the lead. To make matters worse, I hit the upright, from a penalty kick. At half-time, then, the Rovers were 1-0 in the lead. Was this to be another Walsall?

It was not. For the second half, I took Bobby Davidson's place at inside-right, and Bobby, who had been having an unhappy game, played on the left wing. Our attack, which had already been presented with quite enough chances to have been in the lead, suddenly found its shooting boots. I struck my best form, and wiped out the Rovers' lead with two quick goals. The Bristol side lost heart, and Arsenal ploughed through the mud of the heavy pitch, to add three more goals.

After the game, Mr. Allison wrote a letter to my mother, telling her how proud she could be of her son, who had saved and won the game for Arsenal. It was a nice, if somewhat flamboyant, gesture, and Mother was touched by it.

We were again drawn away in the next round: for the sixth time in a row! This time, we had to visit Liverpool: a tough assignment. We rose to the occasion, however, although an injury to centre-half Herbie Roberts meant that Norman Sidey, the reserve pivot, had to take his place. Norman, by the way, was the only member of our eleven in that match who was not an International! 2-0 we won that match. Let W. M.

Johnston, "Recorder," of the Arsenal programme, supply the commentary on it:

"The Liverpool Cup-tie of 1936 will go down in Arsenal history as one of the most glorious performances. Victories, it is true, have been gained with some regularity on the Anfield ground by visiting Arsenal teams, and it is again true that the actual score on this occasion was not an exceptional one. But nevertheless the triumph was complete and outstanding. Liverpool rose to considerable heights, and their performance was probably one of the best efforts they have made for some time in a Cup match. But in spite of this excellence they were well and truly beaten, and eclipsed in every department. The form of our team, severally and collectively, was superb and would probably have accounted for any team in the land. Each player produced his best form and the combination of the team was magnificent. It was most decidedly our best performance of the season, but we may go further and say that we would have to search a long way before we found so convincing a display."

There you are, then! Curiously, perhaps, this is not a game which has stuck very hard in my memory. Our first goal was scored by Ray Bowden, after fifteen minutes. Alex James sent me away on the wing, I crossed the ball into the goal mouth, and Ted Drake headed it down for Bowden to beat Riley, the Liverpool goalkeeper, with a first-time drive. A quarter of an hour from the end, Ray made a great run down the left wing, finally crossing the ball for Joey Hulme to volley into the net.

For the next round, we were drawn away yet again – this time, to Newcastle United. Never before had we beaten the United, and to make matters worse, Ted Drake had to drop out of our team with a knee injury. Ray Bowden moved over to centre-forward, I came in to the inside-right position, while Pat Beasley took my place on the wing. We held the Magpies to a 3-3 draw on Tyneside, and beat them 3-0 at Highbury the following Wednesday: a game in which I scored a penalty goal, thereby partially atoning for my miss at Bristol.

Barnsley were conquered 4-1 at Highbury, and for the Semi-Final we were drawn against Grimsby Town, at Huddersfield. It was a dour, hard game. Grimsby were all out to lower our colours, and played very keenly indeed, inspired by the leadership of Jackie Bestall, their clever inside-left. For the third Semi-Final in succession, I scored what proved to be the vital goal. I received the ball from centre-forward Ray Bowden, and shot hard for goal, from just inside the penalty area.

George Tweedy, the Grimsby goalkeeper, picked the ball sadly out of his net. It was the only goal of the game. Grimsby never gave up trying, despite being in arrears, and it was a thankful Arsenal team which walked off the field at full-time; victors by one goal to nil.

As usual we trained at Brighton for the Cup Final, which was to be against Second Division Sheffield United. A few days before the match was due to take place, Mr. George Allison called me upstairs to his office. "I'm playing Ted Drake centre-forward," he said. "What do you think about it? I know I'm taking a chance."

"You certainly are," I told him. "I should keep the same team, if I were you. Ray Bowden is doing very well at centre-forward, and I think playing Ted is too great a risk."

However, play Ted did. It was his first game for many weeks, and it was only quite recently that he had come out of hospital, after a cartilage operation. Ted's inclusion was a bitter disappointment to young Pat Beasley, who thereby lost his place. Pat may not have been a great footballer, but he was – and is – a ninety-minute trier, and at that time he was worth his place in any side. Four years previously, he had a chance of playing in the Final, but Joe Hulme had passed a fitness test, at the same time as Alex James had failed his.

We did not give a good display in the Final, and I will admit that we were lucky to get through. Certainly, we had played far better in the 1932 Newcastle match. Ray Bowden was a failure at inside-right – really not his proper position – and was very seldom in the game. One can sympathise with him, as he had been leading the Arsenal attack for a considerable period, and there is a vast amount of difference between the two positions. Herbie Roberts and Alex James had only just recovered from injury; Alex was rapidly approaching the end of his great career; while Eddie Hapgood was worried about his sick mother.

Sheffield almost scored in the first minute when Alex Wilson, substitute for the injured Frank Moss, who was never again to wear an Arsenal jersey, dropped the ball. Fortunately for Arsenal, Alex then proceeded to make a save which was quite as remarkable as his mistake. Sheffield had quite as much of the play as we did, and were definitely unlucky when a header from Jock Dodds struck the cross-bar.

The only goal of the match came sixteen minutes from the end. I beat my man on the left wing, and put the ball across for Ted Drake to score. It might be argued that Mr. Allison's gamble was justified, in that Ted, heavily bandaged, did score the only goal of the game. But if our original formation had been adhered to, I am sure that we would have won far more easily and convincingly. Ted himself was not expecting to be selected, and it would have been a far less bitter blow to him than it was to Pat Beasley, had he been passed over. Pat was destined to play in the Cup Final and gain an International cap with Huddersfield Town and, no less than thirteen years after the 1936 Final, to win a Second Division Championship medal, as left-half and captain of Fulham.

As I have said, Arsenal were lucky to win that day. Yet we had been infinitely more unlucky in 1932, and after all, who were we to worry about the way we had won? The Cup, after all, was ours! We rejoiced accordingly.

17

THE SCENE CHANGES AGAIN

Season 1936-37 saw Arsenal win nothing – not even the F.A. Charity Shield, for Sunderland, the League Champions, beat us 2-1 at Roker Park, in a game in which I was not playing. This was the first time since I had been at Highbury that we had failed to gain any honours. In 1931-32, of course, we had been runners-up for the Cup and the League, but even then we had beaten West Bromwich Albion 1-0 for the Charity Shield: a game, incidentally, in which I scored the only goal.

1936-37 was not a very good season for me, for I received grave trouble from my ears. This trouble began during 1936, but it was then only slight. The right ear only was affected, there being just the merest suspicion of anything amiss with the other. The following year, however, I caught influenza. It was a severe attack, and had a serious effect on my ears, although, happily, I was by no means deaf. I was very worried as to whether I would keep my hearing, and perhaps things appeared worse than they really were. I had not experienced the last of my ear trouble, but never again was I to have such a severe ordeal from them.

What with influenza and my worrying, I very nearly had a nervous breakdown, and there is no doubt that my illness had a grave effect on my play. Before it, I was capped against Wales and Ireland, but afterwards, I lost my place in the England team, and with it, my chance of going on tour to Scandinavia.

One of my most vivid memories of that 1935-37 period, when Arsenal strove in vain for the League – though possibly we might have striven a little harder in the tail end of the season we won the Cup! – was a match we played at Birmingham, against Aston Villa. It will always be remembered as Ted Drake's match. Ted was pitted against the Welsh International Griffiths; a centre-half he always enjoyed meeting. Griffiths was essentially a ball player and an attacker, and he used to find it difficult to counter Ted's vigorous methods. On that particular day he found it quite impossible! He was constantly being caught too far up the field, after a Villa attack had been broken up, and since the Villa backs – as they always have done and still do – were playing much too square, Ted had a picnic. Even if Griffiths did happen to be on the spot when Ted received the ball, he could do little about it. I sensed that it was Ted's day, and, from my position at inside-left, banged the ball up-field to him, whenever it came my way. Ted responded in amazing fashion. He could do nothing wrong. Of the nine shots at goal he had that afternoon, seven entered the Villa net. Of the others, Morton, the Villa goalkeeper, pushed one terrific drive onto the bar – though I don't think he knew very much about it – and the other tore into the side netting.

The curious thing was that Ted was not bothering to get within normal shooting distance. He was letting fly from twenty-five and thirty yards: and almost invariably with good effect. It was a truly remarkable performance.

It was made even more remarkable by the fact that the Villa had almost as much of the midfield play as we did. In fact, if they had had Ted and not us, perhaps they might have won 7-1! I have known many curious matches, but never one quite like this. It was a very great triumph for Ted, who equalled the League scoring record by Ross of Preston North End, set up in 1888.

I spent much of the 1936-37 campaign as Arsenal's right-half. This prompted an irate Arsenal shareholder to demand of Mr. Allison at the annual meeting what he meant by turning the best outside-left in the country into a half-back! As a matter of fact, I was playing in that position at my own request! During October, 1936, Arsenal had been going through a lean period. I suggested at a team conference that the fault lay with the wing-halves, who were not using the ball to the best advantage. I volunteered to play right-half in our match on November 1st against the Racing Club de Paris, in order to try to show them how it should be done. My offer was accepted and, for the first time in my life, I became a wing-half-back. I had a successful game in Paris, doing my best to use the cross-field pass which I have always maintained the wing-half is in the best possible position to employ. Perhaps it was this that revitalised an Arsenal team which had recently been rather in need of a tonic, for we won the match, 5-0.

After it was over, Syd Cartwright, a hard-working young reserve half-back who had watched the game, came up to me. "I'm a right-half myself, Cliff," he said, "and how the devil you make it look so easy, I don't know!" The answer I gave him was it is all a question of confidence and positioning. As a wing-half, I have always found that if you use the ball to good enough advantage, the inside forward you are supposed to mark will end by chasing you. I have always liked that position, and maintain that a real footballer should be able to give a good account of himself anywhere on the field: with the possible exception of goal.

There were three distinct phases in the pre-war Arsenal team, while I was at Highbury. The first, as I have already pointed out, ended with the death of Mr. Herbert Chapman, and saw the arrival at Highbury of Jack Crayston, Ted Drake, and company. This second phase ended around the period of the 1937-38 season. Once again, new faces began to appear, and by the time that season was over, Eddie Hapgood and I were the only men who had been regular first teamers during my first four seasons at Highbury.

The most noticeable departure was that of Alex James, who retired in 1937. Filling the breach was not easy. I would go farther, and say it was an impossible task, which was not, in fact, accomplished. George Drury came to us from Sheffield Wednesday, at a £9,000 fee, and played a number of games for us at inside-left. George, fair-haired, stocky and hard-working, was unfortunately a temperamental and, therefore, inconsistent type of player, unable to maintain for long the form he sometimes showed.

Another who was tried in Alex's erstwhile position was Leslie Jones, the Welsh International inside-forward who came to us from Coventry City, in exchange for Bobby Davidson. Leslie too was inconsistent, and he never really gained a regular first-team place. He did not stay long at inside-forward, but took over from Wilf Copping, at left-half.

Herbie Roberts, thanks to a severe injury, sustained towards the end of the previous season, was also no longer with us. Into his place came the giant, fair-headed amateur, Bernard Joy. Bernard had formerly played in London amateur football, for the Casuals. He had been captain of the British football team which appeared in the 1936 Berlin Olympic Games, and had been England's centre-half in the International that year against Belgium, in Brussels. Bernard was one of the very few amateurs who really made the grade in first-class football. He had patterned himself on Herbie Roberts, but never quite succeeded in inspiring the same confidence among his Arsenal colleagues, although many a time his long legs saved the day for Arsenal, when all seemed lost. He was excellent in the air: but not so great as Herbie, or even Jack Crayston. He was a powerful, rugged tackler, but there again, with Bernard, there was always, to my mind at least, the gnawing fear that he might make a slip – although he seldom did. Bernard was one of the finest amateurs ever to gain his place in a professional side, and I suppose it was his misfortune that he had to bear comparison with such a magnificent predecessor as Roberts.

Once I have been asked how Bernard went down with the rest of the Arsenal team. Was there any feeling over the fact he, an amateur, was keeping out a professional, who would otherwise have played? Let me say at once that no such thought even entered our heads. Bernard, a grand, likeable fellow, was always one of us. This schoolmaster centre-half, who now delights readers of the London *Star* with his well-informed football articles, never really reached greatness, perhaps, but he rendered magnificent service to Arsenal.

Joey Hulme was another who dropped out of the Arsenal side. He remained in the game, however, joining Huddersfield Town. In the 1938 Cup Final, it is interesting to note that he and Pat Beasley formed for Huddersfield a pair of ex-Arsenal wingers.

Joey's place was ultimately taken by Alf Kirchen. Alf had joined us from Norwich City, in 1934, at the recommendation of the Norwich manager, who was none other than our old skipper, Tom Parker. Hulme's consistent form had kept Alf out of the Arsenal first team, although he had made spasmodic appearances, but during the 1936-37 campaign he came to stay for keeps, and was selected by the F.A. for England's Scandinavian tour.

Alf was a player of the Ted Drake type; big, fast, and hard-shooting. He was equally at home on either wing, for he could hit a ball left- or right-footed, with equal facility. On his day, he could be one of the most dangerous wingers in the game. I say, on his day. Consistency was not Alf's strong point: but nor had it been Joey Hulme's, before him. He would have been an even finer player had he possessed a better idea of positional play, while he was always unsure when to carry on with the ball himself, and when he should flick it inside. He played some of his best games when I was his inside or half-back, and was able to shout, "Inside, Alf!" or "Take it on!" according to the demands of the situation.

Alf and I were – and, for that matter, still are – very good friends. Besides having attained international class as a footballer, Alf is a magnificent rifle-shot. I must confess that some of the stories he would tell me about his prowess with the rifle were hard to believe, and I came to regard him as Arsenal's Baron Munchausen! That was until I went out shooting with him one day, on a farm. A covey of six pheasants was put up. In a twinkling, Alf had accounted for two which were nearest to him, and as the others were flying away he bagged two more of them. Off the football field, I do not profess to know much about shooting, but to me, Alf's achievement seemed quite remarkable. Ever since, I have looked upon him as an Annie Oakley, rather than a Munchausen, and have credited the tales of his exploits accordingly!

When Alf stayed with me in Devon we would drive across the moors in the gathering dusk of a summer's evening, and he, sitting on the sunshine roof with his rifle, would merrily take pot-shots at the rabbits which frisked about in the gloaming. Alf, whose career was unhappily cut short by injury, is now a highly successful farmer in Norfolk. As a matter of interest, he and I nearly went into partnership on a farm in the early months of the recent war, before he had joined the R.A.F.

Besides an outside-right, centre-half and inside-left – also a left-half, when Wilf Copping rejoined Leeds United – Arsenal also acquired a goalkeeper. The passing of Frank Moss left a serious gap. Alex Wilson filled it for a time, then George Swindin joined us from Bradford City. Since the end of the war, George has made terrific strides. Before it, however, he was not particularly impressive. He was inconsistent and excitable. One could not rely on him when he came out to gather or challenge for the ball. His goal-kicking was very poor. Now, however, his kicking is infinitely stronger, his handling of the ball is excellent, and he is a master of angles: particularly when an opposing forward comes through on his own, with only George himself in the way. George covered himself with glory on Arsenal's 1949 tour of Brazil, and added another League Championship medal in 1947-48 to the one he had gained ten years earlier. Not a great goalkeeper, perhaps, for he was never able to eradicate a tendency to make the odd elementary blunder, but a good footballer, for all that.

New faces were appearing in many other teams, besides Arsenal's. Much was being heard from Wolverhampton of the exploits of a new young centre-half, by name Stanley Cullis. In Liverpool, the Everton fans were talking about Tommy Lawton, the young centre-forward who had been brought from Burnley, with the ultimate intention of taking over from the great Dixie Dean. Ring out the old, ring in the new. A new era was beginning.

Wolverhampton Wanderers came very much into the picture in 1937-38, so far as Arsenal were concerned. We put them out of the F.A.

Cup, and just managed to beat them in an intensely exciting race for the League. Our Cup-tie with them is very green in my memory. It was a Fourth Round game, and the week before it was due to take place Arsenal ironically had to play the Wolves at Molineux, in a League match. We lost, 3-1, which did our League aspirations no good. I myself was not playing.

During the ensuing week, L. V. Manning, football columnist of the Daily Sketch, wrote an article in which he said that, if I was declared fit, I could beat the Wolves on my own. He even forecast the way in which I would do it! Morris, the Wolves right-back, would, he said, concentrate on keeping me out on the wing. In his anxiety to prevent me from cutting-in, he would leave me plenty of room to slip by him on the outside, and it would be from my resultant centres that Arsenal would score the goals which would reverse that 3-1 decision.

I was passed fit for the game, my injured ankle yielding to the ministrations of Tom Whittaker, and travelled with the rest of the team to Wolverhampton. As I came into Tom's room in the hotel where we were staying – a regular ritual with Arsenal players on the eve of any away match – I was greeted by a chorus of, "Here he comes! This is the man who's going to beat the Wolves!" from the other lads who were gathered there. Curiously enough, L. V. Manning's prophecy turned out to have some truth in it.

Straight from the kick-off, I raced down the wing with the ball, beat Morris on the outside, and centred for Ted Drake to lunge the ball past goalkeeper Scott, with his shin. Wolves fought back, however, and little Bryn Jones equalised with a superb header. Wolves pressed our defenders very hard indeed at times, but our rearguard was very much equal to the occasion, particularly Bernard Joy, whose fair head was bobbing up whenever the ball sailed into the Arsenal goal mouth, while Eddie Hapgood obliged with yet another of his goal-defying kicks off the line. Eventually, Alf Kirchen sealed the issue for us, with a second-half goal from an almost impossible angle.

I had a good match, and had a very favourable Press after it. Most of the sports writers took the view that Arsenal's win was attributable to me – though this was something of an exaggeration. L. V. Manning was almost patting himself on the back, as he travelled home on the train to London, in the same carriage as the Arsenal party. "What did I tell you?" he would ask us, at frequent intervals. "Didn't I forecast what was going to happen?" He had certainly been right to a large extent, for Morris, a good back, against whom I usually seemed, however, to do well, did concentrate a little too much on crowding me out on to the left touch-line.

Not all professional footballers liked L. V. Manning, although I myself got on with him well enough, and was deeply sorry to hear the news of his death in a motor accident in April 1946. Yet although I liked L.V.M., it was easy to see why so many players didn't. He was something of a sensationalist, and inclined, I thought, to be far too severe. Footballers, after all, are only human, and it is unfair to blame them too harshly for an isolated bad game. Besides this, I considered L.V.M. particularly callous towards young players who fared badly in their first International. Often, his words had a hurtful effect, which I'm sure he did not intend, and would not have brought about, had he appreciated the harm a few unkind words can do.

We went out in the next round of the Cup, losing 1-0 at Highbury to Preston North End, the eventual winners. We were more successful in the League, however, although at one time it looked as if we had no chance at all of success. We started well enough, but the team went into a bad patch, and at one period we sank as low as eleventh. That was in November, but a fortnight from the end of the season we were fighting out the Championship with Preston and the Wolves, and a great 3-1 victory at Preston put us into first place. We were two points ahead of Preston, but we only led Wolverhampton by goal average; and they had a game in hand.

Our win at Preston, who were top of the table before the game, was largely due to a grand performance by Eddie Carr, our tiny reserve centre-forward. Eddie headed a goal from George Male's centre, early in the game, and scored another, later on. Thus we took some measure of revenge for the Cup-tie defeat Preston had inflicted on us three months earlier. A curious feature of the game was that Alf Kirchen received a violent kick on the knee, and benefited from it! Before the injury, he had been unable to bend his leg back to its full extent, thanks to a previous knock. After he had been kicked, he found the leg was all right again! It's an ill wind...

The following Saturday we met Liverpool, at Highbury, and squeezed through by the only goal of the game. Again Eddie Carr was our hero, for he it was who scored it. Wolves, meanwhile, could only draw at home with Chelsea, who thus did us a really good turn, while Preston dropped out of the race by failing again. Two days later, Wolves played their game in hand, beating West Bromwich Albion in a local Derby at Molineux, by the odd goal of three. They were ahead! One game to play, and the Wolves were on top with 51 points, we were just behind them, with 50!

The last day of the season came round, after that seemed an eternity of waiting. Arsenal were to play Bolton Wanderers at Highbury. We were determined that nothing should stop us that day, and the Arsenal Stadium was a torrent of raging sound, when Alf Kirchen crashed the ball past the Bolton goalkeeper, to give us the lead. Two more from Eddie Carr, and we were ahead at half-time by 3-0. Anxiously we waited in the dressing-room for the interval score at Roker Park, where Wolves were battling it out. It came, and was read out. Sunderland 1, Wolves...0! We knew then that we would be Champions. Even if Wolves forced a draw, we would beat them by virtue of our superior goal-average, and it was a happy Arsenal team which trotted out for the second half. We scored twice more – both goals going to me – and finished winners by five goals to nil. Then the news came through that the one goal of the game at Roker Park, scored by Horatio Carter, had proved too much for Wolverhampton. We were Champions for the fifth time in eight seasons, and I was to receive my fifth League Championship medal.

Up the Gunners! It was destined to be our last major honour, before war swept over Europe.

18
PERSONALITIES I KNEW

During my long Football career, it was my privilege to meet scores of famous men and women, and even to know some of them intimately. Space does not permit me to recall every one of them, but in this chapter I shall discuss a selected few, all of whom stand out vividly in my memory.

First on the list is Ralph Reader – a man who will need no introduction to those conversant with the London theatre. Ralph, of course, is a talented producer, and is particularly famous for his "Gang Shows". During the war, when he was in the Royal Air Force, these shows were made up of members of the R.A.F., but they actually originated with Boy Scouts – a movement in which Ralph has long taken a keen interest.

I got into touch with him when he invited me to take part in a Football Quiz at a Scout Troop in which he was interested. After that, we saw a great deal of each other, and I spent many happy hours at his Scout Gang Shows which, to my mind, were quite as good as, and often better than, any costly production in the West End of London. Like Ralph himself, all the scouts concerned in the shows were really grand fellows, and excellent company.

It was Ralph who initiated me behind the scenes in the fascinating world of Show Business. In the words of the popular song, "There are no people like Show people." They are a happy, genuine, casual crowd, who populate a world which is definitely their own – a world of bright lights, grease paint, "difficult" audiences and variety agents – a world in which, like that of professional Soccer, everything is rosy once you have reached the top, but disillusionment and bitter disappointment so often wait the young aspirant.

Through Ralph Reader I became acquainted with the Hale family. I knew Binnie Hale particularly well. Binnie, red-headed, talented and vivacious, was then – and, indeed, still is – utterly unspoilt by her success. She comes from a remarkable family. Bobby Hale, her father – now, alas, no longer with us – was perhaps the most colourful character of them all.

I first met him when he was playing in pantomime, at Golders Green. Ralph and I saw the show, then went behind the scenes to

Bobby's dressing-room. Bobby gave us a hearty welcome, like the genial soul he was. "Why don't you go along and see Sonny and Jessie?" he asked, after a while. "They're playing in *Hold My Hand*." Sonny and Jessie, it should be explained, were, respectively, Sonny Hale, Bobby's son, and Sonny's wife, Jessie Matthews. "They'll be glad to see you," continued Bobby. "Sonny's a quiet boy: he hasn't got much to say for himself. Still, you'll like him."

So off went Ralph and I to the West End, where *Hold My Hand*, a great London success at that time, was playing. We waited until the interval, and then went behind the stage to see Sonny and Jessie. Almost as soon as we had entered the door, Sonny began talking: largely about himself. As far as I could see, he did not stop until it was time for him to go on stage again. Ralph and I were in that dressing-room for a good quarter of an hour, and I don't believe either Ralph or I opened our mouths once!

I liked Sonny – and Jessie too. But I have a sneaking feeling that Bobby Hale was pulling our legs when he told us Sonny was a quiet lad!

I knew most of the famous stage and screen stars in England during the nineteen-thirties. The celebrated partnership of Bud Flanagan and Chesney Allen, Charlie Kunz, the pianist with the master touch, Anna Neagle, and her film-producing husband, Herbert Wilcox – both of whom are great Arsenal supporters – and many more besides. One of the few I did not meet but wished to, was Gracie Fields. Yet perhaps it was well that I did not. When Gracie was introduced to Alex James – at a time, mind you, when Alex's name was a byword all over Britain – she asked airily: "And what does he do? Ride a bicycle?" Alex, who usually had plenty to say, was rendered speechless!

On the sporting side, perhaps the most famous character with whom I was well acquainted, outside football, was Fred Perry. Fred did quite a lot of training at Highbury, under the eagle eye of Tom Whittaker, at a time when he was losing form. Thanks largely to Tom, he regained it, and went on to add fresh laurels to a great tennis career.

I well remember meeting Fred after watching him play in a tournament in Torquay, shortly before he turned professional. I had brought a couple of friends along with me, both great tennis enthusiasts, and both rather disappointed at the performance Fred had put up that day. "I'm surprised at you Fred!" I told him. "I brought my friends all the way from Exeter to see you play, and they're thoroughly disappointed. I think I could have beaten you myself!"

Fred, who was clad in immaculate evening dress at the moment, raised his left hand, and carefully touched the first fingers of his right hand, and then his shoulder. "From there to there, Cliff", he said, "is worth £30,000. What would you have done?"

It was the first intimation I had had that Fred was considering giving up his amateur status. "You go ahead and accept the offer, Fred," I advised him. "You've done your stuff for England. Now do something for yourself."

Soon afterwards, Fred turned professional. For his sake, I was glad. But on my own behalf, I was a trifle sorry. For Fred had promised to give me some tennis lessons, shortly before he left for America. I am still waiting for them!

I always found Fred eminently likeable. It was a pleasure to watch him on the court; I saw him play at Wimbledon on many occasions; and off it he was grand company. He may have made enemies, but I think that was largely because of the jealousy bred by his successes.

And now for a greater personality, perhaps, than any of those I have already mentioned: this time, a man inside football. I am referring to Harry Homer, the world's champion football supporter: better known to Arsenal fans as "Marksman".

I first met Harry when I was touring Europe with the England team. He was, and indeed still is, dominated by a passionate love of football amounting almost to a monomania. No football match that Harry wanted to see was too far away for him to see it. In his time, he has travelled thousands and thousands of miles all over the Continent, getting from one football stadium to another. Harry was the fortunate possessor of a private income, which enabled him to satisfy his craving for Soccer – but only up to a point. Until that point, all was well. He would travel in first-class railway carriages, rolling across the Continent in ease and comfort. But when that point had been passed, and Harry's travelling expenses exceeded allowance – that was where the fun started! From the first-class carriage, poor Harry would gravitate to what was little better, if at all, than the cattle truck. At times, he would hitch-hike. At others, he would merely hike! We of the England parties became quite used to seeing him stagger up to our hotel, Tyrolean fashion, with a knapsack on his back, and bare knees!

The first time he visited my home at Exeter, however, Harry gave mother a shock. When she opened the door, to find a bare-legged, haversacked young man standing on the doorstep, she did not know whether to faint, or ring up the police! Fortunately, she did neither, and Harry has been a welcome visitor at Exeter ever since.

Harry was Arsenal – as well as England-mad, and I was responsible for introducing him to the authorities at Highbury. He became assistant honorary secretary of the select Arsenal Club Enclosure, and when W. M. Johnston, the secretary, died, Harry took over his post and, with it, the editorship of the Arsenal Programme. He was really in his element.

Like his predecessor, Harry was an Oxford Graduate, and he fully maintained the high standard that Mr. Johnston had set. Under his able guidance, the Arsenal Programme was peppered with erudite references, and many an Arsenal supporter was initiated into the world of English Literature while waiting for a match to begin. During the close season of 1949 the programme was revised, and Harry is no longer in charge.

We had some epic nights together, on the Continent. Besides his many accomplishments – among them being fluency in half a dozen different languages – Harry was capable of drinking ten strong men underneath the table. I think he was born out of his period, for he is an Englishman out of the true Elizabethan mould; the kind of whom Shakespeare has said: "He drinks you with facility your Dane dead drunk; he sweats not to overthrow your Almain; he gives your Hollander a vomit, ere the next pottle can be filled."

I hope Harry will forgive me for trespassing on his preserves, but I could not resist the quotation!

To close this chapter, I would like to deal briefly with my film career. Oh, yes! I have been an actor, too!

The start of my epic screen career was a film called *The Unlucky Number*. Subsequently its title was altered to *The Lucky Thirteen*: presumably to placate the gods! It was, as my readers may have guessed, a picture with Soccer at its theme. The star part was played by Clifford Mollison, while Eddie Hapgood, myself and one or two other Arsenal players lent a hand, on day-to-day expenses. Alas, there was no five-figure contract for me! Co-starring with Clifford Mollison was Gordon Harker, who, not unnaturally, played the part of a detective.

Clifford may have been a good actor, but he certainly had very little knowledge of football, and some amusing incidents resulted. On one particular occasion, he turned up at Highbury for some film shots, intended for the role of an experienced League star, with a brand-new pair of football boots! "That's out!" said Eddie and I, and fixed him up with a pair which had been broken in.

When the script called for shots of Clifford in action, the legs were those of either Eddie or myself. For one scene, however, in which he had to be fouled, Clifford had to do the job himself; and it was a job which did not particularly appeal to him! The "fouler" was to be our reserve left-back, Tommy Black, whose task was to trip Clifford up as quietly as possible, whereupon grounds for the foul would have been given. But Clifford wasn't playing! He ran up the wing with the ball, and then, as Tommy moved in, he jumped straight into him, instead of waiting to be tackled! Tommy was knocked out, and the scene had to be shot seven or eight times before Clifford could be persuaded to stay put!

The greatest surprise I had about the film was provided for me by Gordon Harker, however. On the set, Gordon spoke with the acute Cockney accent that he always adopts in films. Imagine my surprise, then, when he turned up to watch the shooting at Highbury speaking in a faultless Oxford accent, immaculately dressed, even down to a large pair of spats; the whole picture completed by a little dog, which he held on the end of a leash!

The second film I made was also the biggest: *The Arsenal Stadium Mystery*. Based on the book by Leonard Gribble, the cast included, besides the Arsenal players, Leslie Banks and Esmond Knight, who had made such a magnificent recovery, after being blinded in the sinking of H.M.S. *Hood*.

The film featured a match between Arsenal and a legendary amateur team, the Trojans. For goal-mouth scenes, the parts of the Trojans were taken by members of the Cambridge University Football Club, but the long-distance shots came from actual matches at Highbury. Payment was good for the Arsenal players, although the film company tried to suspend it, when production was held up for a period.

The third and last film in which I was involved was *One of our Aircraft is Missing*. This concerns the crew of an R.A.F. bomber, who bale out over enemy territory, during the recent war. One of them is a famous footballer, and in the scenes shown of his career the legs belonged to me!

So much for my filming career: brief, but most interesting. A tailpiece to it is that I have never seen any of the three pictures in which I took part. Perhaps it is just as well. I might have become convinced, when I saw myself on the screen, that I was destined for a cinematic career, and followed it, in preference to football!

19
MY LAST TOUR

At the end of the 1937-38 season I was selected by the F.A. for my fourth – and what transpired to be my last – international tour. I had previously been with the England team to Italy, Switzerland, Hungary, Czechoslovakia and Austria: where we had gone down by two goals to one in 1936. Now the England side was to visit Germany, Switzerland and France. I had already played in the last two; for England against the Swiss, five years previously, and several times in Paris, for Arsenal against Racing Club de Paris. The German match, in particular, was arousing a lot of interest in England. The international situation was tense, and it was known that the Germans were all out to beat us. Their team included most of the players who had appeared against us at Tottenham, two years previously, when I scored one of England's goals in an easy 3-0 win.

When the England party arrived in Berlin a shock awaited me. I had been led to believe that the city was a purgatory of militarisation and uniforms, and, with memories of Rome in 1933, I had vivid pictures of what I would see. To my surprise, I hardly saw one uniform, throughout the time I was there. Perhaps the Germans had taken them off for the occasion of our visit, as a security measure! Or perhaps the reason was that Hitler, who was out of the city at the time, had taken the bulk of the uniformed goose-steppers with him.

Curiously enough, the German hospitality was excellent: even though our dressing-room quarters were situated hundreds of feet above ground-level! There must have been a large amount of anti-British feeling, whipped up by the Nazis, in Berlin at that time, but if there was, I, for one, did not notice any.

There was a huge crowd of 110,000 Germans in the splendid Olympic Stadium when we took the field. Before the match started, both the English and the German teams gave the Nazi salute. Personally, I did not feel very strongly about the incident. We had been requested to give the salute by the British Ambassador, in accordance with the insipid policy of appeasement, which was being pursued by the British Government, at that time. We gave our own salute immediately afterwards, and it seemed to me that this palliated any indignity that there might have been in stretching our right arms in the Nazi fashion. If we had been requested to give the Nazi sign alone, then I would have been angry. Certainly, the German crowd appreciated our action. They cheered us to the echo.

The much-vaunted German team proved to be a moderately good side, but I thought their standard considerably below that of other Continental teams which I had met. My partner at inside-left was West Ham United's Len Goulden. The last time I had played with Len was in a schoolboy international match, a dozen years before! Eddie Hapgood captained the England team, from his usual position at left-back.

The match was played in terrific heat, and an odd feature was the garb of the referee. He wore leggings, and a cloth cap! Neither of these facts upset us, however, and we won with something to spare.

I scored our first goal after sixteen minutes. The German goalkeeper punched out a cross from Stanley Matthews. I caught the ball on the volley, with my right foot, and flashed it into the net. It all looked so easy that the German crowd gave us an admiring cheer.

Three minutes later, Germany were practically presented with the equaliser, when one of their forwards was left unmarked at a corner. They were, in fact, virtually given all three of their goals. Three more goals brought the score up to 4-1 in our favour; then, in the second half, during most of which I was limping, Gauchel, their centre-forward got a second for Germany, when Vic Woodley missed the ball at a corner. The third German goal came when the ball bounced off Ken Willingham's studs, to their outside-left, but meanwhile we had notched a fifth, and Len Goulden completed the scoring with the kind of goal everybody wants to get: a terrific volley from long range, which the German goalkeeper never saw.

The sensation of the match was Jackie Robinson, of Sheffield Wednesday, our inside-right. Playing in his first International, at the same age I had played in mine – nineteen – he ran circles round the German defenders.

Aston Villa's Frankie Broome put in a usual performance for us at centre-forward, then turned out for Villa, who were touring Germany, the following day, in their match against Greater Germany. Frank was in great form at outside-right, his normal position, and played a large part in Villa's excellent win. There was some trouble at this match, for the Villa team refused to give the Nazi salute, and the crowd gave them an unfriendly reception. In their return match with Greater Germany, Villa did give the salute, were cheered by the crowd – and lost!

From Germany, we went on to Switzerland, where we were to meet the Swiss in Zurich. This turned out to be a game which I would like to forget. Conditions were hardly in our favour. It was a small ground, with the spectators crowding to the verge of the very touch-lines. To make matters worse, a boy's match was played on it just before our own. This churned up the turf considerably. It is a villainous habit, this playing of "curtain raisers" before a big game. The only playing which ought to be allowed on the football pitch before an important match should be provided by the band.

The Swiss virtually kicked England off the field. It was quite the "dirtiest" game that I have ever been unfortunate enough to play in. Stanley Matthews was regarded as the danger, and perhaps it was not purely coincidental that he was injured, early on. The Swiss, who adopted the five-in-a-line forward formation, with the wing-half-backs marking the opposing wingers, and the full-backs looking after the centre of the field, took the lead after half an hour. Amado, their captain, who had formerly played for Tufnell Park, in English amateur football, sped past Eddie Hapgood and Don Welsh on the left, and outside-left Aeby headed the ball past Vic Woodley from his centre.

Five minutes later we were awarded a well-deserved and overdue penalty. I took it, and scored. It was another penalty, awarded eighteen minutes from time, that won the game for Switzerland. Poor Alf Young, our centre-half, gave it away. A month before, he had conceded the Wembley spot-kick which had resulted in George Mutch giving Preston North End victory in the last minute of extra time, in the Cup Final. It was not altogether certain whether that was a penalty, and Alf will swear to the end that the foul given against him in Switzerland was non-existent. Certainly, it looked quite an accident when the ball bounced up and hit him on the arm. The linesman on the spot did not think that this was intentional on Alf's part, but unfortunately the referee did. Abegglen, Switzerland's much-capped inside-right, scored from the penalty.

We received a lot of blame from the English Press for losing that game, but I thought it blame that was unfairly apportioned. The nature of the ground and the unfairness of the Swiss tactics were strongly against us. Besides, it is too seldom taken into consideration that England teams go abroad after a long and weary eight month season. How can they be expected to reach their best possible form? I have found that when

England lose abroad, they are damned categorically; when they win, it is taken for granted.

From Switzerland, we went on to Paris, for what was my twenty-first – and last – international. The England selectors made some rather curious team changes; but they were effective. Stanley Cullis, Wolverhampton Wanderers' centre-half, came in at left-half, in place of Don Welsh. Frankie Broome, our centre-forward, became outside-right, while Stanley Matthews, always a right-winger, took over from Jackie Robinson, at inside-right. Ted Drake, the third Arsenal man in the party, filled Broome's place at centre-forward.

The plan was for Frankie Broome and myself to lie back, in order to draw the French wing-half-backs out of position. Meanwhile, Frankie and Stanley Matthews would interchange constantly, over on the right wing.

After only five minutes, the plan brought a goal. Right-half Ken Willingham put the ball out to the right wing, where Stanley Matthews had taken Broome's place. Stanley sent the ball inside to Broome, who dribbled his way through the French defence, to give us the lead.

It was an exciting game, although the football never reached the standard it did in Berlin. Unlike the Swiss, the Frenchmen allowed us to play football. Len Goulden and I had a rather successful partnership together, on the left wing.

Soon after our goal, a shot from me hit the post: which was the signal for three goals in three minutes! Jordan, the French centre-half, came up to head into the England net at a corner. Meanwhile, Vic Woodley was being bundled into the net without the ball: a fact which did not seem to worry the referee.

Ted Drake, who was having some terrific tussles with Gusty Jordan, an old rival in Arsenal-Racing Club encounters, restored our lead. Almost immediately, Nicholas, of Rouen, the outstanding goal scorer in French football at that time, beat Woodley with a terrific, curling shot from thirty-five yards out.

But there was no stopping Ted Drake, who throughout the game was at his dynamic crashing best. He took a pass from Len Goulden, dashed through for goal, and got his foot to the ball just before the French goalkeeper could reach it. Slowly, it trickled over the line, to give us a 3-2 half-time lead.

The second half was mostly England, and we should have increased our score considerably – yet we only got one goal, and this came from a penalty! Ted Drake was badly fouled in the penalty area, and I took the spot-kick. I slammed it past the French goalkeeper, left-footed. It was my twelfth and last goal in International football.

So, at the Colombes Stadium, on a summer's day in 1938, the curtain went down on my England career. It had been a good game for me: and for Arsenal. Ted Drake and I had, between us, been responsible for three of the goals, while Eddie Hapgood, behind us, had played a faultless game at left-back. England 4, France 2. It was a happy English team that sailed back to Dover.

20
MARS INTERVENES

On an August day in 1938, Arsenal Football Club presented Wolverhampton Wanderers with a cheque for £14,000, and Brynmor Jones, all five feet six inches of him, became an Arsenal player.

No transfer before or since has attracted so much comment with the possible exception of Alf Common's, when he joined Middlesbrough from Sunderland, at the first £1,000 fee. Before Bryn's transfer, the record fee had been a mere £10,890, paid by Arsenal to Bolton Wanderers for David Jack, who would have been cheap at twice the price. Could a footballer be worth as much money as £14,000? People asked themselves. And even if he could, was Bryn Jones in particular worth such a vast amount? Would he be affected by the huge fee paid for him? These and many other questions were debated daily in the public-house and in the Press. Indeed, echoes of them persisted right up to the very day when little Bryn left Arsenal, in 1949, to coach Norwich City.

I myself thought at the time that this was a bad transfer, and subsequent events did nothing to alter my views. But it was not so much on account of the price that I was not enamoured of the deal. My objections to it were founded on the nature of the player himself, rather than the vast amount that was paid for him. I had played against Bryn in both club and international matches, and had thus had ample opportunity to size him up. To my mind, he was essentially an attacking player, who was successful at Wolverhampton very largely because the rest of the team was playing well. The wing-half-backs were particularly efficient: so much so that Bryn was having the ball taken up to him: he did not have to go back to forage for it. Bryn, in fact, was just a cog, albeit a highly efficient cog, in the well-oiled Wolves machine. Mr. George Allison, however, wanted to cast him as the successor to Alex James. Well, both were little men; both were inside-lefts, and both were Internationals. But there the similarity ended.

Bryn just did not have it in him to become the general and prime mover of the Arsenal attack. One cannot, in all fairness, blame him. He never pretended to be anything but an extremely efficient attacking player. What Mr. Allison obviously had in mind was that Alex James, too, had been an attacking player, before he joined Arsenal from Preston. Yet Alex had made the grade: why not Bryn?

I could have told him why. Firstly, Alex, even when at Preston, showed signs that he was a real footballer, with a first-class constructive brain. True, he was primarily a dashing goal-scorer then, but a really shrewd judge of football could detect in some of his touches the presence of exceptional scheming ability. The same could not be said of Bryn.

Secondly, if Mr. Allison intended to change Bryn's method of play, as Herbert Chapman had changed Alex's, then he should have asked himself whether Bryn was the type who could weather the bad patch which was bound to be caused by the transition. It was as much a psychological as it was a football problem. Alex, one of the most self-confident persons I have ever known, had successfully weathered the storm: though there was no denying that the storm had been a severe one. Would Bryn stand up to adversity, as Alex had done? Either Mr. Allison decided that he would, or he had not given the matter any thought. As it was, Bryn didn't.

Quiet, modest and self-effacing, he possessed none of Alex's almost aggressive self-esteem. Bryn, alas, proved a failure. It was not his fault. He was, as I have said, never cut out to take over the job which Alex had done superlatively well. With Alex in the team, I was the attacker, and he was the man whose passes kept me, and the rest of the Arsenal line, on the move. Bryn proved a very different type of partner. It was his natural instinct to play as far up-field as I. Arsenal's attempt to curb that instinct failed. So much for little Bryn Jones, a man who would have been infinitely happier if he had never left Wolverhampton.

Season 1938-39, which was, did we but know it, to be the last full-scale campaign for over seven years, was not a distinguished one, for me or for Arsenal. Arsenal finished fifth in the League, and went out in the first round of the Cup, at Stamford Bridge. I had more trouble with my ears, lost form in consequence, and with it my place in the England team. To make matters worse, I developed stomach trouble in the latter half of the season. The doctors diagnosed duodenal ulcers, and I was forced to spend several weeks in hospital. Had it not been for my hearing trouble, I feel confident that I would have managed to keep my England place, right through the war.

In June 1939 I was married. I first met my wife-to-be in the players and officials section of the Tottenham Hotspur Ground. She was Joan Swears, the daughter of one of the keenest and most influential Arsenal supporters, Major Swears; who did, and, for that matter, still does, travel with Arsenal to a great many away matches. I came to know

Joan better at an Arsenal dinner, and the better I knew her, the better I liked her! Eventually, true love ran its course, and we were married: one of the most sensible things I have ever done! I could not have wished for a finer wife than Joan. In the dark days of the war, when things were not going so well for me, she proved a constant source of strength and encouragement. Today, I frankly confess that I should be lost without her, as, too, would Pat and Barbara, my two little daughters.

Hardly had I completed my honeymoon than Mr. Neville Chamberlain announced that he had at long last committed Britain to war with Germany. Almost immediately, the sirens gave us the first sample of the horrible cacophony which was to become almost a theme tune in the south of England during the following year.

Competitive football, of course, was scrapped, *sine die*. I took the blow with philosophy. Frankly, I was feeling rather grateful to be alive. Perhaps it was the gas-mask drill which all Britain had recently been forced to undergo, but to me the sirens that poisoned the ether of a fine Sunday morning in September signified only one word: GAS! Visions of hundreds of Nazi bombers dropping their vile load upon London rose up before me, and Joan and I rushed round the house, sealing all the windows, and blocking up the fireplaces with cardboard!

The Arsenal Stadium, scene of so many epic battles and memorable triumphs, suffered the indignity of being converted into an A.R.P. post. Tom Whittaker became Post Warden, and most of the Arsenal players, including myself, became junior wardens, under him. We were not denied our football, however. A new team, known as the "Arsenal Arps", was formed, with Tom Whittaker as its dashing centre-forward, and Harry Homer on the left wing. Tom showed that none of his old footballing skill had left him with the years, by scoring five goals in a single game. Harry may not have been a born footballer, but he possessed a colossal turn of speed, and I am quite convinced that only the railings which surround the Arsenal playing-pitch prevented him from finishing some of his thrilling runs half way up Highbury Hill!

One by one, the rest of the Arsenal boys were called up for military service, until only George Male and myself were left: George, because he was rather older than the others; I, because my defective hearing rendered me unfit. The two of us went round to other Civil Defence stations, giving the men their physical training instruction, while we also refereed a Civil Defence football tournament, played at Highbury, in which the team that we trained won.

Being a warden was not easy work. Ultimately, George Male was called up for the Royal Air Force, but I stayed on for several years more at Highbury. For most of that time, I was on alternate twenty-four-hour duty; not the best training for playing professional football. I don't know why, but little seemed to happen around Highbury when I was on duty. I was not there when a sacrilegious German incendiary bomb dropped on the Arsenal Stadium, burned out the stand, and set light to one of the goalposts, although I was present when another bomb landed on the practice ground.

Football was soon restarted on a regional basis, and Arsenal, now forced to accept the hospitality of Tottenham Hotspur, at White Hart Lane, won Section "A" of a newly created League South.

It was during 1940 that an Italian news bulletin reported that I was a prisoner-of-war in Italy. I had, so the story went, been piloting an aeroplane over the Gulf or Taranto, in a British bombing raid, when I had been brought down by an intrepid Italian fighter pilot. After my capture, said the report, I had sportingly congratulated the pilot on his prowess! The only thing which rather impaired this story was that I was actually in London at the time it was broadcast!

War-time football was certainly better than nothing, but it was a poor substitute for the real thing. Until about 1943, Arsenal were able to call upon most of their pre-war players, and the guest footballer was a rarity in the team. Most of us were in the services – Jack Crayston, Eddie Hapgood, Alf Kirchen, Ted Drake, George Male and Tom Whittaker in the R.A.F.; George Swindin, Bryn Jones and others in the Army. On the whole, I found war football quite enjoyable.

In season 1940-41, Arsenal had a good run in the League Cup, a competition which embraced all the League clubs in the country. It was divided into regions until its final stages, however, and the ties were played on a home and away aggregate basis.

We disposed of Brighton, Watford and West Ham United, the holders, in the first three rounds; then, in the fourth, we were drawn against the Spurs. This meant that both games would be played at White Hart Lane, which, of course, was a home ground for both of us. Arsenal won the first match, 2-1, before a record crowd of 22,000! When I say record, I am not joking. 22,000 was the war-time limit, thanks to the fear of air raids, and 5,000 unfortunates found themselves locked out, before the start of the game. Shades of 1938, when 75,000 packed White Hart Lane, to watch the Spurs in a Cup-tie against Sunderland!

We won that first leg, 2-1, and I had the satisfaction of scoring our second goal, from a perfect pass from Alf Kirchen. In the replay, all seemed lost, when goalkeeper George Marks failed to put in an appearance. This, however, gave Eddie Hapgood a long awaited opportunity. For many years, he had wanted to keep goal for Arsenal, through the whole of a match, and not just when the actual goalkeeper was injured, as he had done on various occasions. Eddie gave an excellent, if somewhat unorthodox, performance, and we managed to hold the Spurs to a 1-1 draw.

In the Semi-Final, we put out Leicester City on a 3-1 aggregate, winning 1-0 at Tottenham and 2-1 at Leicester – with right-half Jack Crayston scoring in both games. This put us through to the Final, in which we were to meet Preston North End.

This match was to be played outright at Wembley Stadium, and although crowd restrictions were necessarily in force, 60,000 spectators were there to see the fun. It was a match we should have won, but didn't. We had most of the game at the start, and had a wonderful chance of scoring, when Preston gave away a penalty. Had big Leslie Compton, our centre-forward that day, managed to score, I think we would have come out winners. As it was, the best Leslie could do was hit the post, and we rather lost heart, as a result. Andy McLaren put Preston in the lead, and it took us all our time to equalise that goal. Denis Compton was the scorer, thereby making some atonement for his big brother's miss!

For the replay, Leslie Compton dropped out, and Ted Drake took his place at centre-forward. Poor Ted! This game at Ewood Park, Blackburn, had only been in progress a little while, when he sustained one of the many injuries which hampered him in his career. He hobbled on the wing for a while, and then left the field. The doctors present decided that the situation called for morphia, and consequently injected some into his injured knee. Instead of having a soothing effect, however, the drug increased the pain considerably, and by the end of the afternoon Ted was feeling more dead than alive.

We lost that match 2-1. Personally, it was one which I would like to forget. Thanks to my Air Raid Warden duties, I was tired and unfit, and must confess that I was very much off form that afternoon. This, by the way, was the second and last of the War Cups. From then until the end of the war, the League North and League South Cups took its place, under various names.

The 1941-42 season was another good one for Arsenal. We carried off the London League, and reached the Semi-Final of the London Cup. That, however, was as far as we could get. We outplayed Brentford, our opponents, at Stamford Bridge, but an uncanny display from Scottish International Johnny Jackson, lent by Chelsea, prevented us from scoring. In the replay, I missed a penalty, and we went down by two goals to one.

The following campaign was the last in which the Arsenal team kept together, and it was our war-time hail and farewell. We accomplished the Cup and League double, albeit an ersatz one. The Cup Final, played at Wembley Stadium, was remarkable as being one of the most uneven affairs ever to take place on that hallowed turf. Our opponents were Charlton Athletic. I myself had played regularly through the earlier stages of the competition – which, by the way, was run in the form of four separate leagues, the winners of which went on to the semi-finals – but for the Final, it was rumoured that I would lose my place. Mr. Allison, it was said, was negotiating to include young George Curtis, who was playing brilliant football in South Wales, or Bryn Jones, at inside-left, in my place. These negotiations fell through, however, and although the Arsenal inside-left on the programme was designated as "Jones (B.) or Curtis", it was I who actually played. This was how the teams lined up:

Arsenal: Marks; Scott; Leslie Compton; Crayston; Joy; Male (captain); Kirchen; Drake; Lewis; myself; Denis Compton.

Charlton Athletic: Hobbins; Cann; Shreeve; H. Phipps, Oakes; Davies; Revell; Mason; Welsh (captain); Brown; Green.

Almost immediately, Reg Lewis put us ahead. Denis Compton scored a second after eight minutes, but Charlton reduced the arrears from a penalty, after Laurie Scott had dived to fist out a shot which had beaten George Marks. That was the beginning and the end of Charlton's participation in this game. We scored two more goals before half-time, and finished winners by seven goals to one!

Although I myself had expected that we should beat Charlton, I had never anticipated that we should rattle up such a terrific score. Our powerful forward line was the chief reason for our success. Ted Drake fitted in perfectly with Reg Lewis, as an attacking inside-forward; Alf Kirchen and Denis Compton were constantly dangerous on the wings, while I stayed in the rear of the other four forwards, and plied them with passes, in the accepted Alex James fashion. Our goals, by the way, were scored by Reg Lewis, who netted four times, Ted Drake, twice, and Denis Compton.

It is interesting to note that, two years previously, Leslie Compton had played in the Wembley Cup Final as a centre-forward, whereas in this game he appeared as a left-back. Of the Charlton side so thoroughly overwhelmed that day, no blame could be attached to goalkeeper Syd Hobbins, who joined Millwall, in 1948. Jimmy Mason of Third Lanark, the only guest player on either side, has, of course, won much fame of late, as Scotland's inside-right.

As winners of the South Cup, we met Blackpool, who had done the same thing up North, at Stamford Bridge. There were only five Blackpool players in the Blackpool side! This was their star-studded team: Savage (Queen of the South); Pope (Hearts); Hubbick (Bolton Wanderers); Farrow; Hayward; Johnston; Matthews (Stoke City); Dix (Tottenham); Dodds; Finan; Burbanks (Sunderland).

We started that match as if Blackpool were to be another Charlton. Within a quarter of an hour, Reg Lewis and Denis Compton had beaten Savage. Then Blackpool scored an extraordinary goal, which took the heart out of us. Ronnie Dix, a rival of mine in schoolboy days, took a speculative and seemingly useless shot, from fully fifty yards. It was obvious what he was going to do, well before he shot. Somehow or other, though, George Marks, our goalkeeper, missed the ball, and it ended in the back of the Arsenal net. Before half-time, Eddie Burbanks had obtained Blackpool's equaliser. It was a really fine goal. Eddie rang rings around Laurie Scott, before slamming a terrific shot past Marks.

The second half was largely Blackpool. Eddie Burbanks, now with Raich Carter's Hull City, proved too good for Scott, while Leslie Compton had a nightmarish afternoon against Stanley Matthews. Jock Dodds gave Blackpool the lead, with a shot from an "impossible" angle, and Finan rubbed it in, with a fourth goal. Perhaps the score rather flattered them. We had our chances in the second half, and Alf Kirchen made a great effort, fully deserving a goal. Ted Drake did not come off so well as an attacking inside-right as he had done in the match against Charlton, however, which partially explains our defeat. But if Ronnie Dix had not scored that goal...

During the war, several young Arsenal players came into prominence. Most of them are still very much in the public eye today. There was, for example, George Marks, who took over from his namesake, George Swindin, in the Arsenal goal. Marks, spectacular, courageous, and the possessor of a terrific kick, represented England in eight war-time Internationals. It was in the last of these, against Wales, in 1943, that he received the eye injury that resulted in his loss of form. He is now almost back to his old brilliance with Reading, under the management of Ted Drake, following spells with Blackburn Rovers and Bristol City.

Three Arsenal full-backs made a name for themselves. At right-back, Laurie Scott speedily came to the fore. He had joined us from Bradford City in 1937, but the brilliant consistency of George Male and Eddie Hapgood had prevented him from making a single first team appearance. Laurie, of course, is now an England International many times over. His greatest asset is his ability to recover quickly, and today he is certainly outstanding among defenders. By pre-war standards, however, I do not consider him a great player. His positional play and kicking are both a long way behind those of his predecessor, George Male. To my mind, the test of a great full-back is not so much how speedily he can recover, but how many times he has to do so.

Leslie Compton, tall, good-looking and curly haired, also came into his own during the war. Few people realise that he played his first First Division game for Arsenal as far back as 1932, when he was a lad of nineteen, fresh from amateur football. Leslie, in fact, was given his chance of succeeding Tom Parker, before George Male: but he failed to take it. Ever since I first saw him in action, Leslie has been a good footballer in every way: a clean, powerful kicker; unbeatable in the air; a rugged tackler, and a fine positional player. If only he had a little more speed, he would not have had to spend seven long, loyal years in the Arsenal reserves. In war-time he played most of the first season as a centre-forward. His height, with his consequent ability in the air, coupled with his strong build and powerful shooting, made him a really dangerous leader, and he actually gained a cap in that position, against Wales.

In a match against Clapton Orient, at White Hart Lane, he once slammed home ten goals! Admittedly, the Orient goalkeeper was raw and inexperienced – so much so, in fact, that most shots that went between the posts and under the bar usually finished by hitting the back of the net – but, nevertheless, Leslie's was a remarkable feat.

After 1940, he spent most of his time in his proper position of left-back, where he did so well that he made four more appearance for the England team, and it is odds on that he would never have lost his place, had he not been drafted overseas, in 1944.

Today, Leslie is revered in football as Arsenal's dominating centre-half. Since 1945 he has established himself as one of the outstanding personalities of post-war football, and although he is ten years older than most of his opponents this difference in years never seems to make any adverse difference to him. Possibly he has been helped by the fact that the centre-half position does not call for as much speed as does full-back. Footballer that he is, Leslie seems to be able to make a success of any place on the field. On the first day of the 1942-43 season he kept goal for us at Charlton, when George Swindin did not appear. He played very well there, too!

Walley Barnes is the third of the full-backs to whom I referred. Like Leslie Compton, he can make a success of any position on the field, and, at various times, he has appeared in first-class football as a full-back; either flank; a goalkeeper; a wing-half; a centre-half; and inside-left, and an extremely effective left-winger.

"This lad has got everything," I said to myself, the first time I saw Walley play. He joined us from Portsmouth, in 1944. At the time, he was still an amateur, and guesting with Southampton. Thus, for a £10 signing-on fee, Arsenal robbed Portsmouth of a future captain of Wales. Walley has a fine positional sense, can kick with both feet, and is most reliable in the tackle. My only criticism of his football is that he is a trifle slow in recovery. This is perhaps the one respect in which he is inferior to Laurie Scott, his partner in so many Arsenal matches.

Walley's story is a romantic one. Towards the end of his first season with Arsenal he received an injury which finally resulted in his quitting the game, in 1944. Surgeons told him that he would never be able to play again, but he has fought his way back to fitness, and today must be one of the finest defenders in the world.

Two forwards who had made a few appearances for Arsenal before the war, but really came to the fore during it, were Denis Compton and Reg Lewis. Denis is one of the greatest all-round sportsmen England has ever known, and the £12,000 he recently received for his benefit was no more than he deserved, for his splendid prowess on the cricket field. As a footballer, I find it rather difficult to form an opinion of Denis, for war-time football provided no proper test, and since the war he has not played very much League Soccer. He has a fine left foot, and clever ball-control, and perhaps if he had devoted more time to football, since the war, he would have been able to achieve his ambition of adding a full cap to those he won during hostilities, and in a post-war Victory International. As it is, Denis, quite unspoilt, for all his brilliant success, is undeniably a better cricketer than he is a footballer.

Reg Lewis, who made his first appearance for the Arsenal First Division team in 1938, when he was only eighteen years old, soon showed that he had all the attributes of a born footballer. Ball control, pace, physique were – and are – all his, and it seemed at one time as if he would become the greatest centre-forward Arsenal had ever had. Unfortunately, Reg has never quite fulfilled his promise. Over-elaboration, inconsistency, and a certain lack of energy have prevented him from doing so.

One war-time game in which both Reg and Denis took part, and which I, too, have good cause to remember, took place at Aldershot, in 1942. During the war, Aldershot blossomed from an obscure Third Division side into one of the most powerful combinations in the country. The reason, of course, was that, thanks to the huge army base there, the Town were able to call on scores of first-class players, to make up their team. On this particular day in 1942, Arsenal were heading the League South, but had to make the journey to Aldershot with a weakened team, Bernard Joy being among the several absentees. Aldershot fielded the current Britton-Cullis-Mercer England half-back line, in its entirety, while in the forward line, big Tommy Lawton, at centre-forward, was backed up by Sheffield United's Jimmy Hagan, at that time the England inside-left. Arsenal were soon in trouble, and by half-time we found ourselves 3-0 down. We scored soon after the restart, but Aldershot banged in a fourth, to make the score 4-1.

At this juncture, the Aldershot trainer, who was watching the match in company with our own trainer, Wally Milne, announced his intention of turning on the baths. After all, the game was won and lost: there was little to be missed by leaving it. Twenty minutes later he returned, and asked Wally Milne what the score was.

"Six-four," Wally told him.

"To us, of course," said the Aldershot trainer, nonchalantly.

"No," answered Wally, "to us!"

Within the twenty minutes that the Aldershot trainer had been away, Arsenal had scored five times! We scored a seventh, later on, and thus ran out winners by seven goals to four! Reg Lewis did the hat-trick, and I scored one of our goals myself, direct from a free-kick.

Incidentally, I was playing right-half, that day. It was a really astonishing match. Once we had found our feet, there was nothing Aldershot could do to stop us. Partly, no doubt, our revival was attributed to the fact that Aldershot rested on their laurels, but when they did realise that the game was slipping out of their hands, and tried desperately to save it, we were playing much too well to let them. Had the game gone on another ten minutes, we might have won by 10-4. That was how it was running.

That season was quite a good one for me. Unfortunately, however, the fact that I was in the Civil Defence, and not in one of the services, prevented me from appearing in any of the representative matches which virtually acted as International trials.

Early in 1943 I left my post as an Air Raid Warden, and went to work in a factory, for the first time in my life: the Smith Sectric Clock factory. For the first few days it nearly broke my heart. At half-past seven in the morning I had to clock in. At lunch-time I was obliged to clock-out – and then clock in again. Finally, as a parting gesture, I had to punch the clock as I left for home. And going home was no easy matter. Outside the factory, long queues formed for the buses. When a bus eventually arrived, a mad scramble ensued, in which I, not yet versed to this gentle art of scrambling, almost invariably found myself on the outside, looking in. Oh, the monotony of it! And oh, the wretched indignity of it! At Highbury, I had turned up for training with a heart and a half, but never had I been forced to submit to the dreadful ignominy of clocking-in! For the first few days of my new-found industrial career I began to think along Lord Shaftesbury lines!

Only for the first few days, however. By the end of the week, rather after the fashion of Lord Byron's Prisoner of Chillon, who came to love his gloomy dungeon, I developed an affection for my job! I was an operator on a centre-less grinding machine, and although it necessitated my standing up all day, which was hardly the best training for my football, it proved quite an interesting occupation. For the next couple of years, the wages it brought helped me to eke out the penurious rewards paid to the professional footballer in war-time.

The end of the 1942-43 season witnessed the break-up of the Arsenal team. One by one, almost all of us departed for overseas, or some part of the British Isles which rendered playing for Arsenal an impossibility. For the first time since war started, the guest player began to play an important role in the Arsenal team. Among the many players who wore Arsenal colours as guests were Stanley Mortensen, then fast making a name for himself, by his dashing methods; his future partner at Blackpool, Stanley Matthews, then with Stoke City; Blackburn Rovers' stalwart centre-half, Fred Hall, now doing sterling service with Sunderland; Stoke City's centre-forward, Freddie Steele, now player-manager of Mansfield; Ken Moody and George Tweedy, of Grimsby Town; Les Horsman or Bradford, and many others besides.

Stan Matthews only played one League game for us, but it aroused a terrific amount of attention. He came south on an R.A.F. course, in 1945, and long before he was due to arrive in London there was great speculation as to which London team he would assist, during the week-end he was there. Arsenal, Chelsea, Millwall – all were mentioned, until, with a fanfare of journalistic trumpets, it was announced that the great Stanley had graciously consented to lend his services to Arsenal! Another triumph for Mr. George F. Allison!

So Stan duly turned out for us against Millwall, and the gate, which ordinarily would have been round the 9,000 mark, swelled to the very good war-time total of 21,081. Millwall, our opponents, shook us by taking a half-time lead. Shortly after half-time, however, I sent a cross-pass out to the right wing, and Stanley rushed in to score our equaliser. Subsequently, we added another three goals, one of which went to me, for an easy 4-1 win.

So much for war-time football. As the war drew on, and players went overseas, it grew steadily worse. Crowds were limited – even after the air-raid restrictions had been lifted – and there was a half-hearted atmosphere about most of the games I played in.

But none of these things mattered very much. Nobody ever pretended that war-time football had any real significance. What did matter was that the much-bombed, underfed people of Britain should be given entertainment. This the professional footballer gave them. The average Briton loves the game of football, and I am sure that the fact he was able to see his favourite team in action, even though sadly depleted, throughout the war, was a really important factor in boosting morale. And that was all that mattered.

Timing is the key.

Balance is essential when heading the ball.

F.A. Eleven *versus* Army Eleven at Windsor.

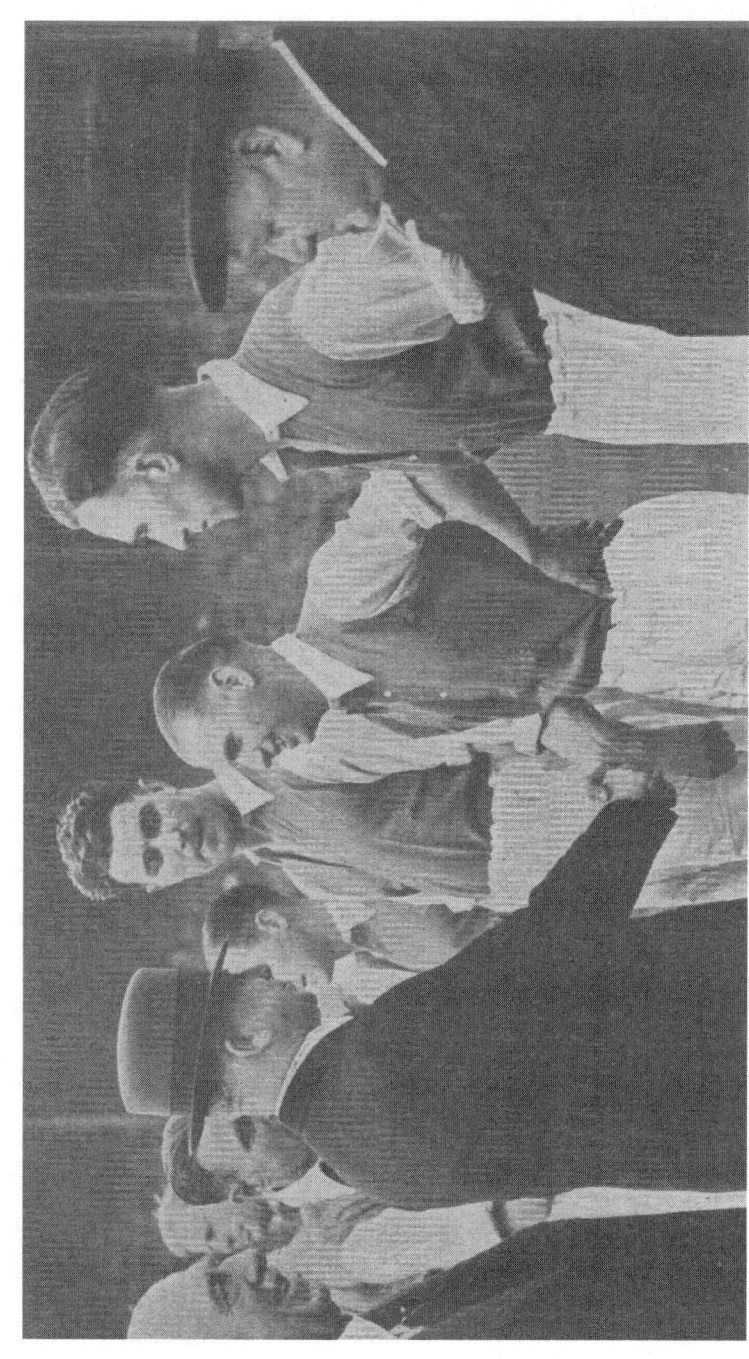

The Rt. Hon. A. V. Alexander shaking hands with the author: Cup Final, Wembley, 1941.

Arsenal team versus Charlton, Cup Final, May 1943.

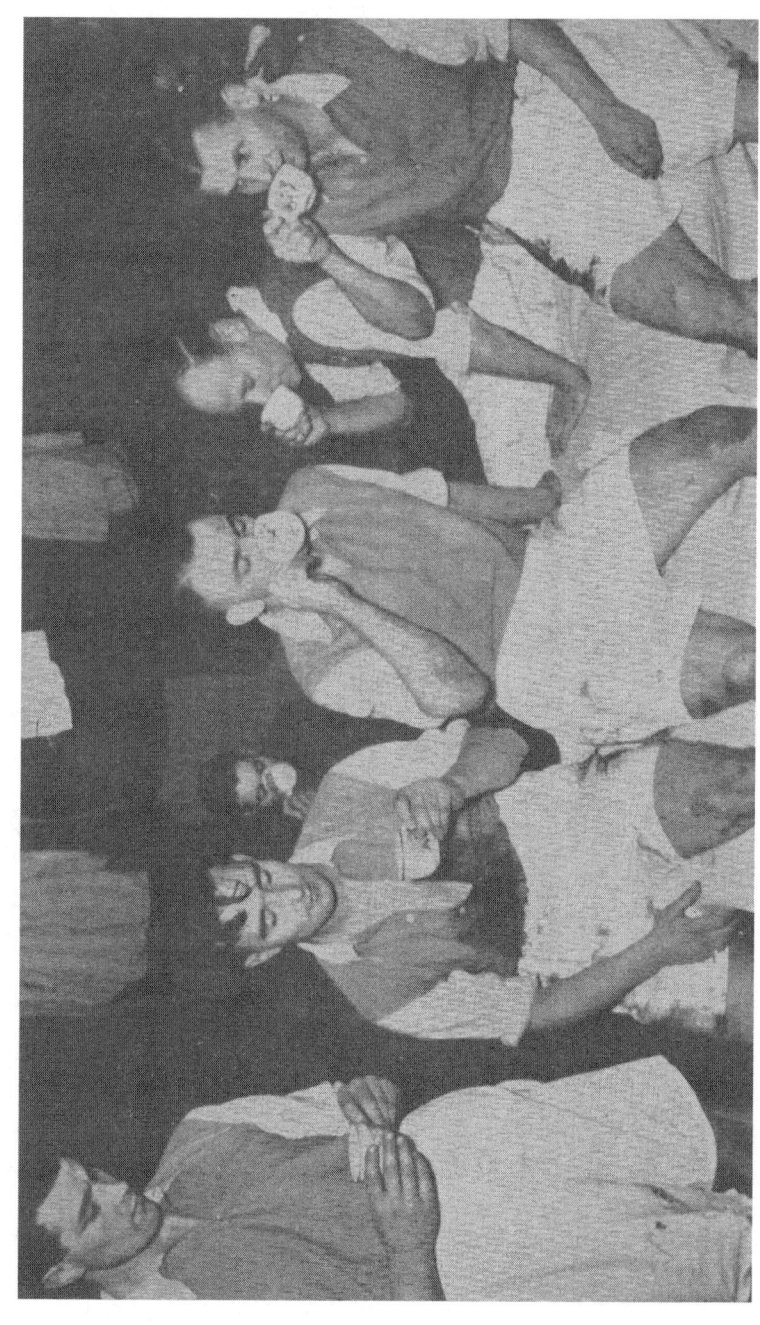

Half-time; The tea drinkers are: L. Compton, D. Compton, Marks, Collett, Male, Bastin.

Tom Whittaker.

A typical scene at the Arsenal ground, Highbury.

21

BLINDMAN'S BUFF AT TOTTENHAM

On a raw October day, in 1945, a party of surely young men stepped out of an airliner, at Heathrow. The Moscow Dynamos had arrived.

No tour in my experience has attracted more interest from the start than that made by these Russians. Before any arrangements had been made concerning their match programme, or even the dates of their visit, they had insisted on meeting Arsenal. This was quite understandable for, although at this particular period we were struggling along with a makeshift team which varied with every match, our name had stood high on the Continent, ever since our great era of the nineteen-thirties.

I was pleased that we were to meet these Russian mystery men, for I was always eager for new experiences in football, and this promised to be something very much out of the ordinary. But my suspicions were roused when the Russians announced that the referee who was included in their party must take charge of this particular game. They appeared quite content to have British arbitration for the matches against Cardiff City, Chelsea and Rangers, and I feared at the time that they regarded the match with Arsenal as being of political rather than sporting importance.

As everybody knows, the Russians drew their first match, with Chelsea 3-3, although they might have won very comfortably, had they only taken their chances. As it was, they were lucky to draw, for their third and equalising goal was blatantly offside. However, the referee, Lieutenant-Commander Clark, allowed it – probably in the good cause of Anglo-Russian friendship!

The following Saturday, the Dynamos defeated Cardiff City by the crushing score of 10-1, and it was obvious to everybody concerned at Arsenal that we were in for a very hard game.

No one appreciated this fact more than Mr. Allison. He realised that if Arsenal fielded their present side it would probably mean another Cardiff disaster, which would be bad for English prestige, unfair to the name of Arsenal – for our team bore little resemblance to a full-strength Arsenal side – and very little fun for the Dynamos.

Accordingly, Mr. Allison invited various well-knows players to reinforce his team. When finally chosen, it read as follows: W. Griffiths (a Cardiff amateur); Scott; Bacuzzi (Fulham); myself; Bernard Joy; Halton (Bury); Matthews (Stoke City); Drury; Rooke (Fulham); Mortensen (Blackpool); Cumner.

In other words there were five genuine Arsenal players in the side. Wyn Griffiths, however, had been playing for us all the season, and anyway could scarcely be termed a Cardiff regular. The team was really a compliment to the Dynamos, and this was Mr. Allison's primary motive in choosing it.

The Russians, however, took one look at the side and said: "This is England, not Arsenal!" Since the team included two Welshmen, in Griffiths and Cumner, this was tortuous reasoning at the best! Besides, high as Mr. Allison's position in Soccer was at the time, I don't think that even he would have claimed that even a virtually representative team chosen by him, however strong it might be, was entitled to carry the label of "England"!

In point of fact, he was justifiably annoyed at the specious way in which the Russians had boosted the merits of their opposition, in order to make quite certain that even if they lost, or drew, they would lose no credit by it. However, judging by subsequent distortions of fact by the Kremlin, I suppose this was a comparatively mild one! But I still feel relieved that Wyn Griffiths and Horace Cumner aren't Welsh Nationalists!

At last, the day of the match dawned. It was what foreigners imagine to be a typical November day in London. The whole city was enshrouded in thick, grey fog. I hoped against hope that it would clear, but by lunch-time there was no sign of any change for the better, and when I arrived at White Hart Lane, Tottenham – which was then, of course, Arsenal's home ground – the Spurs' enclosure was swallowed up in the gloom.

In the dressing-room, I found a miserable bunch of Arsenal – and Arsenal for the occasion – players. There seemed absolutely no prospect of the match being held, and we morosely awaited the inevitable news of cancellation. Still, we thought, we shall probably play the game later in the week.

But, to our utter astonishment, we were informed that the Russian referee, M. Nicolai Latyshev, had decided that the game should take place.

Accordingly, a few minutes before the kick-off time, we trooped on to the field. Perhaps I should say that the Dynamos trooped on. We merely trotted out in the way that British teams always do. But the Russians marched out of the tunnel and into the middle of the field with military precision. There was something unnatural about these young men, who were always so restrained and unspontaneous in their manner.

We lined up before the large crowd – in spite of the weather, nearly 55,000 spectators were present – and the usual introductions took place. I was most disappointed, however, to find that there was going to be no presentation of flowers by the Russians, as there had been in their previous matches. As captain of our side, I was very much looking forward to receiving a huge bouquet of flowers from the dour, rugged Semichastny, my counterpart in the Dynamo team.

I thought at the time that this was a token of the seriousness with which our opponents regarded this match, but discovered afterwards that a presentation had been planned, only to be abandoned because of the unfavourable conditions. The crowd would have been quite unable to see it. So the bunches or carnations were left in the Dynamos dressing-room, and the subsequent tone of the match was indicated from the start.

As we Arsenal players went to our places for the kick-off, we suddenly noticed the curious position taken up by the referee. He had stationed both linesmen on the same side of the field, while he himself was to patrol the other. In normal conditions, perhaps, there might have been something to be said for this system, but in the circumstances, M. Latychev's decision bordered on imbecility. It was barely possible to see farther than ten yards on the field of play, let alone for Latyshev to espy his linesmen, right across the width of the ground.

However, there wasn't anything we could do about it, so we – and the two English linesmen – settled down to make the best of a bad job.

Dynamo started off on the attack, and were very soon awarded a free-kick, inside our half, and on the left flank of our defence. What this kick was awarded for, none of the Arsenal team knew. Joe Bacuzzi was right on the spot, and he was completely mystified by the referee's decision. Be that as it may, Dynamo took the kick, and Beskov, their centre-forward, got on to the ball and scored. It was a very good goal, although, as I have said, the circumstances leading up to it were a trifle suspicious. Wyn Griffiths, our goalkeeper, was kicked on the head in trying to prevent the score, and played for the rest of the half with concussion. In spite of this severe handicap, however, he only let through one more goal.

The first goal came after only thirty seconds play, but we took it in our stride, and Ronnie Rooke soon put in the equaliser. In view of the fact that our team had never played together before, and was recruited from no less than six different clubs, it was displaying astonishing teamwork, and it was no more than we deserved when Stan Mortensen made it 2-1 in our favour.

The Dynamos were disheartened by this reverse, and we began to get well on top. There was no stopping our brilliant forward line, in which Stanley Matthews was giving left-back Stankevitch a terrible time, and Mortensen scored our third.

It was no mean feat to be 3-1 in the lead against this Moscow side, and the achievement was made particularly meritorious by the tactics we had to contend with. I have found all the Continental teams I have played against were very much addicted to obstruction, and the Dynamos were no exception. Stanley Matthews was the greatest sufferer from these methods. Time and again, his shirt was pulled, as he was making tracks for goal, yet Latyshev's whistle never blew.

He was, indeed, not really a referee at all, but a twelfth man on the Russian side. His decisions, when he made them, were quite extraordinary. His pip-squeaking whistle never blew when an Arsenal man was fouled, but if there was the slightest suspicion of a foul on a Dynamo player, he would sound a veritable *obbligato*. The thick, dank fog, which was growing denser all the time gave him the perfect excuse for "not seeing" things he ought to have seen. But it was certainly rather curious how he invariably managed to espy any incident which contained possibilities of a free-kick for the Muscovites!

Five minutes from half-time, Beskov beat the injured Griffiths to make it 3-2.

Half-time came with no change in the score, and it seemed as if Dynamo were booked for defeat. They were playing so badly towards the end of the first half that we might well have been three or four goals in the lead, let alone one. The weather conditions were almost insufferable, and the game should have been stopped long ago – it was folly even to start it. We wanted to turn straight round at half-time, in order to get the game finished while there was still some degree of visibility, but the Russians adamantly refused.

The result was that both teams adjourned to their respective dressing-rooms, while the fog grew thicker and thicker outside.

There was a Russian-speaking Englishman in the Dynamo dressing-room, to make things run smoothly for the visitors, and he declares that he witnessed a cameo more befitting a theatre than a football stadium! When the Dynamo players came off the field, they found eleven cups of steaming tea awaiting them – a regular custom, this, among British football teams, and one which seemed particularly appropriate on this occasion. The Russians, however, took one look at the tea, picked up their cups, and splashed the liquid right across the floor. Then they drank vodka! One can hardly blame them for preferring their own national beverage, but they might have expressed their distaste for ours in a less forcible manner! Still, in view of the suspicious attitude adopted today by Russia towards the West, perhaps the Dynamos' behaviour can be explained. They probably thought the tea was drugged!

While the players were quaffing their vodka, the English interpreter overheard a conversation between the Russian manager and the referee. If the game continued to run in Arsenal's favour, said Manager Yakusin, it should be abandoned. But if Dynamo began to get on top, the referee was to let the game go on.

The authenticity of this reported conversation was borne out during the second half, when the Russians were leading 4-3. By this time, it was virtually a game of blind man's buff, and players on both sides had to rely primarily on guesswork. Mr. George Allison approached the Soviet Envoy and the Dynamo Manager, and asked them if they would agree to the abandonment of the game. It was an entirely justifiable request, for the thickness of the fog and the unscrupulous tactics of the Dynamo defence had reduced the match to the level of a farce. Every time an Arsenal forward penetrated into the Dynamo penalty area he could count himself lucky if he was not fouled. But the only reply to Mr. Allison's request was a Molotovian refusal.

So the game went on. We now had Harry Brown, of Queen's Park Rangers, in goal, instead of Wyn Griffiths. Harry was rather nervous at first, and in the fifty-first minute he fumbled an easy ball, which rolled through his hands and into our net. This should never have been a goal at all, for the Russian outside-left, who made it, was standing yards offside when he received the ball, and the whole of our defence stood still, confidently waiting to hear Latyshev's whistle. We were unduly optimistic, for although one of the linesmen had waved his flag vigorously, the referee took no notice of him at all.

Twenty minutes later, Bobrov got what proved to be the winning goal. This, too, seemed to me a blatant case of offside. The score was allowed, however, and I had the impression that so long as the Dynamos got the ball into the net, even if they carried it there, the referee was going to award them a goal.

Our own forwards were hopelessly situated. The decisions given against them, bad at all times, were sometimes fantastic. Take, for instance, the time that a Russian caught hold of Matthews' shirt – to have a free-kick awarded in his own favour!

As right-half, I was not always able to penetrate the gloom sufficiently to see what was going on in the Russian penalty box, but what I did see was quite enough to destroy my faith in Russian referees for ever and ever! Latyshev had forbidden his linesmen, before the start of the game, to make any decisions with regard to incidents in the penalty area; so he had matters all his own way.

I witnessed two examples of the way he exercised his supreme jurisdiction in the penalty area, and at the time, I did not know whether to laugh or cry!

On the first occasion, early in the second half, Stanley Mortensen went hurtling through the Dynamo defence at terrific speed. It looked odds on a goal, but suddenly a Russian foot stretched out, and Stanley went flying through space. This incident took place ten yards or so from the Russian goal, yet no penalty was given.

On the second occasion, Ronnie Rooke triumphed over adverse circumstances, to score one of the most remarkable goals I have ever seen. I need hardly add that it was disallowed!

It happened like this. Ronnie pounced on a loose ball, and, in his usual manner, went straight ahead for goal. Just as he was about to shoot, Semichastny, the Russian centre-half and captain, jumped on his back! In his desperate effort to rid himself of this Muscovite Old Man of the Sea, Sinbad Rooke swung his arm backwards. There was a satisfying thud, and Semichastny released his hold. Ronnie went on to put the ball into the net.

But the goal was disallowed – and a free-kick awarded to Dynamo! Perhaps there would have been some very slight excuse, had the referee called play back and given Arsenal a foul. But to give a kick the other way...Words fail me!

Semichastny, incidentally, came off the field after the match with a black eye. This he quite correctly attributed to Ronnie Rooke. But his accusations were given a good deal of publicity in the English Press, and he subsequently withdrew them, saying instead that he had suffered an accident in the fog after the game. My own opinion is, that the Russians feared that if he continued with his allegations, the full story would ultimately come out – and it was not a story calculated to show the Dynamos in a very good light.

As if the weird refereeing of Latyshev was not enough, for twenty minutes of the second half the Russians were playing twelve men – or thirteen, if you include the referee! Trofimov, the outside-right, was injured, and Archangelski came on to take his place. All well and good, but Trofimov did not go off! The fog prevented one from seeing very much, but I had a feeling that the Russians had one man more than us, at throw-ins on the other side of the field to my own. Ultimately, Trofimov did leave the field.

At last, the game ended, and the Dynamos had beaten us, 4-3. It was a disgruntled bunch of Arsenal men which left the field side by side with the marching Dynamos. We all felt absolutely certain that in reasonable conditions, and with a proper referee in charge, we would have won convincingly.

But there is no denying that the so-called Moscow Dynamos were a very good side indeed. I say so-called, because information I have received from friends who often visit Russia, and follow Soccer there, has led me to believe that these Dynamos were not a club side at all. In fact, they were virtually the Russian International team. So perhaps our game with them should have been billed, "England *versus* Russia"!

The great strength of the Dynamo team lay in their forward line. Indeed, their attack was so good that it made a moderately competent defence look poor by comparison. The forwards played in a different formation to our own, the centre-forward lying well back, with the inside-men covering the ground that he would cover if he was playing the English type of game. If a long pass went down the centre, both inside-men would run on to the ball.

This formation worried Bernard Joy, our centre-half, who was uncertain which man he should mark.

The two wing-forwards did a good deal of wandering inside; a feature which was often upsetting to our defence: but the great strength of the Dynamo forwards did not lie so much in formation and positioning, as in passing.

They did very little dribbling, preferring to make their way up the field with short, quick passes. Never have I seen a forward line place its passes so accurately as did these Russians. They were especially adept at the pass inside the back to the winger: to my mind, the best move in football. Joe Bacuzzi said, after the match, that the facility and accuracy with which they made this particular pass was quite uncanny. The two inside-forwards, Kartsev and Bobrov, were the men responsible.

Furthermore, I found the Dynamos' speed very deceptive. They were all expert ice-hockey players, and moved with an ease and grace which one associates with skates, rather than with football boots. On many occasions, I would see a Russian player moving towards a ball I was chasing myself, with long, smooth strides; gliding along, at what seemed a comparatively slow rate. It was only when the player in question had beaten me to the ball that I realised how fast he really was moving.

Yet there were several weaknesses in this Moscow Dynamo side, and I do not think they would finish very high in the English First Division, were they to participate in it. Firstly, their defence was not up to First Division standard. Deprived of its obstruction and shirt-pulling, it is far from impregnable, and I was not even impressed by the much-vaunted goalkeeper, "Tiger" Khomich. He seemed to me just another flashy Continental-type goalkeeper, whose chief talent was to make everything look twice as difficult as it really is.

Secondly, the Dynamo inside-forwards did far too much standing about, far up the field, thereby putting an unduly heavy burden on their half-backs. Against a first-class, fully trained English team – remember, the season that the Dynamos came over was transitional – these inside-men would have to come back to assist the defence. This would inevitably deprive them of much of the energy which they expended in their lightening-speed attacks.

They would then be faced with an alternative choice of evils. Either they would have to play the English inside-forward game, which would, of course, mean the end of the attacking scheme which was their greatest strength; or they would tire themselves out, long before the season was over.

It also seemed to me that the Dynamos, in common with all the Continental teams I have played against, possessed no real team spirit. They were a grand side when things were going well, but their individual players did not possess the collective determination to retrieve an adverse situation.

Finally, I found all their players very vulnerable to an English-type shoulder-charge. They did not seem robust enough to withstand it.

I have often been asked what I think would be the outcome, were the Moscow Dynamos to meet the Arsenal of the 1930-38 period. My answer has always been the same. I consider that for the first twenty minutes or so, the Arsenal defence would be a trifle puzzled by the unusual formation of the Russian attack. For that period, play would be fairly even. But by the end of it, the Arsenal defence would have mastered the Dynamo methods, and our forwards would take control. We would then win comfortably, for, as I have said, the Dynamo defence left much to be desired.

I would have liked to play against the Dynamos under conditions more befitting a football match, and at a time when I was at my peak. By 1945, I was almost at the end of my career. Still, the fog farce at Tottenham is quite unique in my experience, and it is some consolation to think that I took part in a game which will certainly go down in football history.

22
MY LAST GAMES FOR ARSENAL

In January 1946 the Football Association celebrated the end of the recent war by staging the F.A. Cup, for the first time since 1939. Once again, the Third Round, and with it the big clubs, took its place in the sporting calendar, although the Football League competition had not yet restarted. There was one important difference from the pre-war tournament: the ties were going to be played on a home and away basis, with the exception of the Semi-Final and Final. Whether the Football Association was justified in restarting its Cup competition so soon after the war is a very debatable question. Personally, I thought it most unfair to those clubs who still had star players serving abroad. Arsenal's predicament in this respect was particularly unfortunate, and will serve as an illustration of how many other clubs found themselves situated.

At the time when we had to meet West Ham United, in the Third Round, such stalwarts as Leslie and Denis Compton, Bryn Jones, George Marks and George Curtis were all overseas. Besides this, injuries during the war period had accounted for Alf Kirchen – who played his last game for Arsenal at West Ham, in 1943 – Ted Drake, Walley Barnes, and Jack Crayston. Alf Kirchen had been severely injured in a collision with a West Ham player, and, but for a remarkably skilful surgical operation on the torn ligaments of his leg, he would have been crippled for life. I am happy to say that Alf has made a splendid recovery. Soon after he had left hospital he bought two Norfolk farms, and, as I have already mentioned, he has become a highly successful farmer.

Jack Crayston had succumbed to ankle injuries, soon after Alf's mishap; Walley Barnes had been out of action since the second match of the previous season; while a heavy fall in a match at Reading, in 1945, had ultimately proved to be the last in Ted Drake's luckless series of injuries. It is curious to reflect that he now manages the team on whose ground this injury occurred.

However, to return to the match in hand; the first of our Cup-tie meetings with West Ham, scheduled to take place at Upton Park, was expected to be a close and exciting affair. Alas for Arsenal, it was nothing of the sort. No Arsenal team I have played in has ever given such a miserable Cup-tie exhibition. West Ham scored two quick goals, and by half-time they were four in the lead. Ultimately, they won 6-0.

Apart from the absence of the players I have mentioned, there were, admittedly, excuses for our very poor show. At half-time, it turned out that all three of our inside-forwards, Lewis, Drury and Henley, were crippled by injuries, while our young left-back, Joe Wade, was forced to be recalled to the side, when he was out of training. The collapse of our defence was largely due to his excusable inability to cope with the West Ham right-wing pair. I myself was playing on the left wing, and found I could not produce the necessary speed for the position which I once had had, thanks to a handicap of which I shall have more to say later. West Ham, to give them their due, did play quite well – but they had very little to beat.

One of the few men to come out of that game with credit was goalkeeper George Swindin – and thereby hangs a tale. On the eve of the match, both George Swindin and George Marks were expected home from the Continent. If Marks had arrived first, it was certain that he would be given preference. He had, of course, been first choice goalkeeper, before he went away. As it was, George Swindin beat him to it, and gave such a brilliant performance that day that he regained his pre-war place, and George Marks was subsequently transferred.

I did not play in the meaningless second leg, the following Wednesday, at Tottenham. We won 1-0, but it was poor consolation for our six-goal debacle at Upton Park.

At the end of that season the Football League was restored: and Arsenal went back to Highbury. On 17th August, 1946, the occasion of our public trial match, an Arsenal team played in public at the Stadium, for the first time in almost seven years. Unhappily, the resources at Arsenal's disposal hardly bore comparison with 1939. Gone were Jack Crayston, Ted Drake, Alf Kirchen, Leslie Jones and Eddie Hapgood. For the match at Wolverhampton, which opened our League programme a fortnight later, we were forced to field a very experimental side, containing only four of our regular pre-war line-up. George Male was playing out of place at left-back; Dave Nelson and George Curtis, pre-war reserve forwards, were our wing-halves; while in the forward line, little Jimmy Logie, Ian McPherson and Paddy Sloan, which last two had joined us in the close season from Notts County and Tranmere Rovers, respectively, were having their first taste of League football. I was on the left wing.

Hardly had that game been in play five minutes, when I realised that my football career was virtually at an end. I had had trouble with my right leg during the previous season, and as I ran after the ball in this match I felt that I was unable to bend it. It was not the knee from which I had experienced cartilage trouble, for that had given me very little trouble since my operation. When I say that my right leg had troubled me the previous season, perhaps I should add that I had had twinges from it even as far back as 1939.

"What is the matter with it?" I asked Tom Whittaker.

"The ligaments may have tightened up through too much playing," he replied.

Drawing the logical conclusion from this, the fact was that I had started my professional career exceedingly early, and in consequence it was finishing early, too: for I was only thirty-four years old at this time.

The half-time score in this Molineux game was 0-0, but George Male was severely injured in the second half, Wolves struck form, and before we knew quite where we were, we were 6-0 down! Just towards the end I put Reg Lewis through, to score a consolation goal for us. Writing on the game, a reporter in one of the Sunday newspapers said: "Bastin exploited his positional sense to the full, but was not so speedy as of yore." Well, now he knows the reason why!

This leg trouble finally decided me on quitting football. Previously, I had given the matter serious consideration, for a surgeon had told me that if I underwent the ear operation, which was likely to prove so beneficial to me, I was certain to be out of the game for at least six months. I reckoned that seventeen years in top-class football was quite long enough for any man, and that I should leave the game before it took leave of me.

But although I was dropped after the Wolverhampton match, I had not yet played my last game for Arsenal. I was recalled after a couple of games, and turned out as right-half and captain at Goodison Park, in a match where Arsenal gave a much-improved display. Unfortunately, we went down to Everton by the odd goal in five, and were thus situated with only one point, and without having won a single game, after four matches. How were the mighty fallen!

But we made a come-back three days later at Villa Park. Ian McPherson, our outside-right, proved far too speedy and tricky for the veteran Scottish International left-back, George Cummings, and we won 2-0, thanks to goals from Reg Lewis, who had thus scored in every game, and Dr. Kevin O'Flanagan.

A word on Dr. O'Flanagan would not be out of place. For a brief period, he was the sporting idol of London. He came over from Dublin, to practise in London, with a reputation as a first-class Soccer player – an International – a dashing Rugby footballer, a sprinter who could do the hundred yards in "evens", a high jumper who had cleared five feet eight inches, and an expert at those tough Irish games of Gaelic Football and Hurling. Otherwise, he didn't play anything at all!

The Doctor was an amateur who obviously enjoyed his game. His dashes down the right wing and the middle of the field were reminiscent of Brian Boroo at his most warlike! I myself always considered the Doctor a Rugby player, rather than a footballer, for although he possessed dash in abundance he did not have very much else to offer. A grand, likeable fellow, Doctor O'Flanagan has unfortunately to some extent been forced out of big Soccer and Rugby – at both of which games he is an International – by pressure of work.

After our win at Villa Park, we scored another away success, this time at Blackburn, against the Rovers, and then opposed Derby County, at Highbury. As a wing-half, I was faced with the inside-forward combination of Raich Carter and Peter Doherty, who had done so much to win Derby the Cup that year, and of whom so much praise had been spoken. They certainly did well against us in this game, which Derby won by the only goal of the match, but I thought they had been overrated. Both of them, particularly Doherty, were inclined to lie well up the field, and not bother to come back in aid of their defence. This led to a terrific amount of work for the half-backs, and had Derby been faced with the pre-war Arsenal forward line, instead of the 1946 edition, I think they would have been badly mauled. Although we lost that match, I enjoyed it immensely – as I did all my games at right-half that season – for wing-half is a position of which I have always been fond.

The following Saturday, I played what transpired to be my last game for Arsenal. It took place against Manchester United, at Maine Road, Manchester, and this was how Arsenal lined up:

Swindin; Male (captain); Joy; myself; Leslie Compton; Logie; McPherson; Sloan; Lewis; Bryn Jones; Nelson.

It would be fitting if I could say that we won that game by a terrific score, with myself outplaying the United on my own, and scoring a double hat-trick. Unfortunately, this was not what happened. Manchester were in good form at that time, and few gave Arsenal any chance of winning. However, we actually took the lead, when I slipped the ball down the centre of the field, through a gap in the United defence. Centre-forward Reg Lewis ran on to the ball, and left Crompton, the Manchester goalkeeper, helpless, with a terrific drive into the roof of the net.

I honestly believe we would have won that match had it not been for an extraordinary lapse by Les Compton, our centre-half, five minutes later. He was strolling after a loose ball, with all the time in the world to pass to Jack Swindin, or even to clear. Meanwhile Johnny Hanlon, the Manchester outside-right, was running along behind him, in what seemed a vain hope that some chance might present itself. It did. Leslie Compton turned right round with the ball, and Hanlon, grateful and surprised, took it off his feet, and walked it into the net. That goal upset Arsenal. We were 2-1 down when half-time came, equalised through a snap goal from Ian McPherson, but subsequently let through three more, to crash 5-2.

After that match I was dropped. I never played for the first team again. Several times I travelled with it, as a reserve, but most Saturdays saw me with no Arsenal commitment at all. On Boxing Day, 1946, I played my last game in Arsenal colours: as captain and inside-left for the Reserve team, at home to Cardiff City. We won 4-0, and I scored one of the goals.

Soon after that game I went into hospital for my operation: and my Arsenal career was over. There was no formal resignation, and no formal notice from Arsenal. Mr. Allison and I just took it for granted after I had entered hospital that I would never play again – and I never did. Like Shakespeare's Othello, my occupation had gone.

23
HINTS FOR THE YOUNG ENTHUSIAST

So many people have written so many words on the subject of how Association Football should be played, that I was a little dubious about including some hints and suggestions of my own in this book. However, I do feel that after more than seventeen years in first-class football I should be able to give some useful advice, drawn from my own experience, to the budding International players of tomorrow.

Firstly, a few words on the subject of kit. Young players are very much inclined to neglect this aspect of the game. Provided they can find themselves a jersey, a shirt, and a pair of boots capable of kicking the ball, they are quite happy. What they do not realise is that the finest of footballers cannot help but lose some of their efficiency if their kit is not in first-class condition.

Footwear should always be comfortable and fully studded. For preference, football boots should, of course, be worn, but this is not essential. Before my parents bought me my first pair of proper football boots, I would hunt out an old pair of boots, and knock studs into them. It is interesting to note that Stanley Matthews played a number of games, during the recent war, shod in Army boots!

I have already mentioned that football boots should always be kept fully studded. Each boot should have four studs on its sole, and two on the heel: one missing stud is enough to throw the foot quite out of balance, besides leading to a great discomfort. Look after your football boots like a new suit! Clean them and grease them after every match – especially if it has been played in wet weather. Unless football boots are kept thoroughly greased, the leather will harden – and this can cause harm to the foot.

Moving a little further up the leg, we come to that very vulnerable part of the anatomy, the shin. Your shins should always be protected. A kick on an unguarded shin cannot only be very painful, but can cause really serious injury. Shin-guards, of course, give the best protection, but failing these, a piece of stiff cardboard cut in the shape of a shin-guard is good enough as a temporary measure. One sometimes finds among youngsters a curious contempt for those who resort to shin-guards for protection. But why? As I see it, there is nothing effeminate or cowardly in taking the trouble to ward off possible injury: it is only common sense.

Continuing with my advice on kit, the next item on the list is the stockings. Football stockings should never fit too tightly. If they do, cramp is liable to result. I have always used string rather than elastic garters, for supporting them, as I find string more easily adjustable. Elastic garters are liable to be too tight, which again can bring cramp to the wearer.

As to the shorts and jersey, there is little to be said. See that the elastic in your shorts is not too tight, otherwise you will almost certainly suffer from the stitch while running: and I need hardly tell you how painful that can be – and what a handicap! Your jersey or shirt should fit loosely, to allow complete freedom of movement.

So much on the subject of kit: what about the game itself? Somewhat naturally, one of the chief objects in Association Football is to kick the ball, yet it is surprising how many aspiring Soccer stars are unable to do this properly. In almost every boy there is the natural instinct to kick a ball, preferably as hard and as far as possible, but so many of them make the little mistake which, though seemingly trivial, prevents them from attaining real strength and accuracy. And don't think for a moment that boys are the only offenders!

Never kick the ball with the toe! Except when making a short pass, the instep should always be used. If you persist in kicking with the toe, it is not only liable to prove quite painful, but you will have no control of the ball. When making impact with the ball – unless it is taken on the volley – the toe should be pointing towards the ground, and the non-kicking foot should rest alongside the ball. A distinction must be made between kicks made by defenders – such as goal-kicks, and long clearances – and those made by forwards.

When making a shot, the forward should only bring back his kicking foot a comparatively short distance, and the actual kick should be a sharp, quick action, with special attention paid to the follow-through. The follow-through is of really vital importance. It is, of course, the essence of almost every ball game, and is just as important to Len Hutton and Henry Cotton as it is to Tommy Lawton. It is useless to stab at the ball hoping for the best. In nine cases out of ten, you will be disappointed.

When a defender attempts a long kick, his foot should be brought back farther than that of a forward, and he should allow his body to slope backwards, when following through. This, of course, ensures that the ball will gain plenty of height: with forwards, the primary object should be to keep it low. Goalkeepers would far rather jump than dive! Note that these instructions on kicking should be followed whether the ball is moving or stationary, provided, of course, that it is on the ground.

Now, a few brief words on the subject of passing. Wherever possible, the pass should be made with the inside of the foot, as this method gives the greatest accuracy. Sometimes a flick with the outside of the boot may be necessary, and for a long, cross-field pass it will naturally be necessary to kick in the normal manner: but use the inside of the foot whenever you can.

Trapping the ball is an art which must be mastered by any aspiring footballer: though it will need plenty of practice to do so. Timing is the secret of success in trapping – and good timing requires that the eye of the would-be trapper should never leave the ball for an instant, until he has it under control. Besides perfect timing, proper positioning and balance are the other necessary qualities. There are three distinct methods of trapping, and I intend to analyse each in turn.

Firstly, trapping the ball dead. The player should get his foot and body right over the top of the ball, as soon as it strikes the ground. As in kicking, the other, non-trapping, foot should be placed alongside the ball. If this position is correctly adopted, the player will be enabled to go ahead with the ball, with a minimum amount of delay.

The second method of trapping, and probably the best, is that of trapping the ball and carrying it on, all in the same movement. The only difference between this and trapping the ball dead is that, instead of trapping the ball with the sole of your foot, the side of the boot should be used. The ball will come to rest a few feet from you, and you can then run on to it quite easily. This move, however, must be carried out with the greatest accuracy, or the ball is liable to run on to an opponent.

The third, and certainly the most difficult, method of trapping the ball is to raise the foot to meet it, waiting until the ball strikes the instep, then bringing the ball down to the ground with it. The most perfect of perfect timing is needed to carry out this method, and I would suggest that the three different ways of trapping should be learnt in the order in which I have set them out.

Leaving the subject of trapping, I now wish to go on to that of heading the ball. This Soccer art is often sadly neglected by amateur players: many try to head the ball; few head it correctly. Never try to head the ball with the crown of your head. The ball is most unlikely to go where you want it to, in the first place, and in the second, you are likely to contract a headache! The proper way of heading the ball is with the top of the forehead, just where the roots of the hair begin. Once again, timing is the secret of success. Watch the ball like a hawk, and at the moment of impact jerk your head, to achieve power; but jerk it to the side, and not downwards. To impart direction to the ball, a twist of the head will do the trick: to the right, if you want the ball to go that way, and, similarly, to the left, if you want to send the ball the other way.

Very often there will be an opponent trying to head the ball, as well as yourself, and the ability to win duels in the air is essential to defenders, and most important to attackers, as well. The secret of success in such duels is to time your jump so that you are in the air just that split second before the other fellow. I scored many a goal this way, myself. Your eye must never leave the ball for an instant, and you must gauge just when and where it is going to drop.

I need hardly say that the standard of heading in British professional football has been for a long time – and, for that matter, still is – at a very high level. Everton's Dixie Dean scored more goals with his head than any other forward in first-class football. Tommy Lawton, his successor in the Everton team, and now captain and centre-forward of Notts County, has continued in the Dean tradition. Watch how Tommy leaps for a high centre: he always seems to be up to the ball before the other fellow. Arsenal's centre-half, big Leslie Compton, is also adept at the timing of his jump, while for the jerk of the head which gets real power behind the ball, there is no better present day exponent than Neil Franklin, the Stoke City and England centre-half. Much helpful information can be set down on paper, but it does simplify matters enormously to see the teacher's maxims actually put into practice. So if Lawton, Les Compton, or Neil Franklin happens to be playing around your district, it would be well worth while for you to go along to see how they deal with the ball when it is in the air.

The next phase of the game I want to deal with is the tackle. Always keep your eyes on the ball – and not on your opponent; otherwise you are liable to be deceived by a body swerve. Try to get both feet in front of the ball, but don't jump at your opponent, for then you will give away a foul. Once again, balance is of great importance. If you keep it, you will be able to recover quickly, and have another try at making a tackle. Brain, not brawn, is the essence of good tackling. Never make a despairing rush or lunge at an opponent, but time your tackle to the most split of split seconds. That was how Eddie Hapgood achieved his tackling: and, to my mind, there has never been a finer full-back.

Now, a word about the throw-in: and it is a word addressed not only to wing-halves, but to forwards and full-backs as well. The importance of the throw-in is not always realised. A quick throw-in, cleverly placed, can very often lead to a vital goal being scored.

To throw a ball in correctly, the hands should be placed behind the ball, so that your two thumbs are touching. Stretch your arms as far as they will go, without discomfort, then bring them back – with the ball, of course! – over your head, at the same time bending the knees slightly. Then raise your arms, releasing the ball just before it comes on to a level with your head, and follow through with your arms, after you have released it. The secret of the long throw-in is to get your hands well behind the ball, in the manner I have just described, and to bring the arms back over the head as far as possible. Don't forget that part, at least, of each foot must remain on the ground.

With plenty of practice, it is not difficult to acquire a long-distance throw-in, but in your exuberance at being able to hurl the ball vast distances, don't forget that the short throw-in can sometimes be more valuable to your side, if taken quickly and correctly. During my career as a winger, I threw the ball in quite as often as did my half-back, and my quickness in doing so often took my opponents by surprise. To make the short, quick throw-in a success, one golden rule must be remembered. Never, never, never throw the ball straight to your colleague! Always throw that yard or half a yard either way, so that he is able to run on to the ball. In other words, look for the open space! This advice, of course, applies just as much to passing as it does to the short throw-in.

Next, I want to deal with a subject which will really be of interest to wingers only: corner kicks. Personally, I always made my corner-kicks in-swingers. In other words, I took them on the left wing, with my right foot. I consider an in-swinging corner preferable at all times to a kick which swings away from the goal. The ball should be hit with the instep, with the body leaning slightly backwards. This ensures that the leg will have the necessary follow-through after impact, to loft the ball into the goal mouth. Try to make the ball drop by the far goalpost, about six yards out from the goal-line. This is a difficult ball for a goalkeeper to field, while your fellow-forwards can rush on to it, as it curls inwards, thereby making his task doubly difficult.

Now, the penalty-kick. I took a great number of these, during my career in first-class football. Some I must confess to missing, but I managed to convert the majority. Riveted to his goal line until the ball is kicked, with a hundred and ninety two square feet of fresh air to defend, the goalkeeper does not appear to have much chance to speak of: yet every week one reads of penalties missed by professional footballers! Why? Well, granted that the odds are strongly in favour of the penalty-kicker, one must not forget the psychological aspect of the situation. Even where a match has no spectators, the player taking the kick has all the twenty-one other players watching him, while in a really important game there may be anything up to a hundred thousand spectators looking on with the greatest interest! In the heat of action, when the ball is in play, even a hundred thousand onlookers can be forgotten. But when the ball is dead, and you are one of the central figures in a little footballing cameo, then it is not so easy!

When taking a penalty, then, you should always try to keep your mind on the job. If the steeplejack looks down, he may turn giddy and fall, and the penalty taker is almost certainly doomed if he lets his mind wander to the outlying circumstances of the situation. Always take your penalties with a plan. It is useless to dash up to the ball, and then either kick it aimlessly with your utmost force, or make up your mind where to place it, at the last moment. Always keep the ball low: the goalkeeper has twice as much chance with a high shot. Aim for one or other corner of the goal and, at the moment of impact, see that your eye is on the ball. The goalkeeper can't move until you have kicked it, so there is little to be gained by watching him. The stronger the kick, of course, the better: but, in this case, accuracy is far more important than mere power.

Finally I come to the subject of positional play. This aspect of the game is so vitally important that I have purposely left it until last, so that I can lay the utmost stress upon it. During my playing career, it was often stated – rightly or wrongly – that I excelled at the art of positional play, and I was frequently asked how I managed to attain such a high standard. The only answer I can make is that it came to me naturally, but that does not mean that a positional sense cannot be acquired, with diligent practice and effort. I have always maintained that a really good positional sense is the most important attribute in any footballer's make-up, so the practice and effort I suggest will be infinitely worth while to any budding footballer. Here, to help him, are one or two useful hints.

The first essential in becoming a really fine positional player is to be on the alert the whole time. Watch the play, whether it is a hundred yards away from you, or whether you are actually in the thick of things. How often does a forward find himself off-side simply because he has not taken the trouble to keep an intelligent eye on the trend of the play.

Secondly, you must try all the time to think just that one move ahead. If, for instance, I was playing for Arsenal, and Joey Hulme was about to lob in a centre from the right wing, I would try to anticipate just where that centre was likely to drop, so that I could rush in on it like a flash, surprising the back who was marking me. Note from this example that thinking one move ahead means trying to anticipate what members of your own side are going to do next, as well as your opponents.

Thirdly, always try to take up position where you are likely to be the biggest nuisance to the other side. For defenders, this is largely a question of being in the right position to cut out passes – vitally important to full-backs, especially. For forwards, the main idea should be to move constantly into the open spaces. The great winger, the late Alex Jackson, of Huddersfield Town, Chelsea and Scotland, was always at his most dangerous when he was without the ball. One never knew where to find him. Like the Scarlet Pimpernel, you sought him here, there and everywhere, and he always contrived to pop up just where he was least expected. Wingers and centre-forwards particularly should try to follow Alex's example. It is the surest way to throw a defence into a panic.

The wide-open spaces, beloved by cowboys, are, as I have said, also to be sought by forwards. When a colleague gets possession, make for the open space as fast as possible, so that you are in a good position to receive the ball. How often have I heard a player barracked from the terraces, for allegedly holding the ball too long, when in reality it was the fault of his colleagues, who will not make for the open space!

By way of an example to illustrate my advice, let me describe how I myself took up position, when playing on the left wing. As soon as the game started, I stationed myself about ten yards inside from the touch-line: I have always maintained that a winger is virtually out of the game if he spends his time positioned on the touch-line itself. Those ten yards of ground gave me numerous advantages. No matter how awkwardly the ball came in my direction, the odds were always on me reaching it, rather than the full-back. More important still, I was in a position to cut through on the inside, and go straight for goal – a nightmare of a move to any full-back. Throughout any and every game my object was always, by intelligent positioning, to make my opponent do what I wanted him to do: never to let him dictate the run of the play.

One last word on the subject. As a forward, I always had a pet theory, and I pass it on to my readers, in the hope that it may be of some benefit to them. "It is better to take up the correct position for a shot at goal six times – and miss five of them - than never to be in the right position at any time." In other words-

> 'Tis better to have loved and lost,
> Than never to have loved at all.

And with that fine, poetic flourish, I shall close a chapter which I sincerely hope will be of much benefit to the aspiring young enthusiast.

24

FOOTBALL TODAY – AND TOMORROW

Often since my retirement I have been asked how I think British Soccer today compares with its pre-war counterpart. I am not able to give a very encouraging answer. Though fully conversant with the fact that distant fields look greenest, I am bound to admit that the standard of football today is infinitely lower than it was before the war.

Since I left the game, in 1946, I have been a sports writer with the *Sunday Pictorial*, and have kept well inside the game in which I was once a participant. Nobody, then, can rebuff my allegations by saying that I have been out of football since I retired. Seldom indeed has it been that I have not spent my winter Saturday afternoon at one professional game or another, but I have yet to see a team which consistently serves up football of a standard comparing with that before the war. Oh yes, I have seen plenty of speed. There is no denying that professional football has become a great deal faster, of late. But is mere speed a worth-while substitute for thoughtful, intelligent constructive play? Is any purpose served by rushing about a football field at immense velocity, only to send the ball, when at length one does part with it, straight to an opponent, or alternatively to a man less well placed than oneself? Surely both these questions must be answered with a very emphatic negative.

If any reader is still ready to debate this point with me, let him look at the number of veterans who are holding their own today, in first class football. Since the end of the war, men like Raich Carter, Joe Mercer, Leslie Compton, Pat Beasley, Len Goulden and Freddie Steele have not only kept their places in League sides, but have actually been among the stars of the post-war period. "You're carrying on for a long time," I recently remarked to a very famous veteran international. "Why not?" he rejoined. "It's just too easy playing, these days!"

Nobody will convince me that a player can improve after he has reached the age of thirty-five. Inevitably, he must start declining. The number of successful veterans in the game at the moment is thoroughly indicative of its low standard. In the craze for speed, speed, speed at any price, these men just stroll through match after match, using their heads and letting the ball and the other players do the running around.

What is the cause of the decline in British football? The answer, I think, is quite obvious: the war. During the war, those young players who should have been brought along gradually by their clubs were obliged to spend their time in the Services. The consequence is that the clubs have had to force into League football youngsters who, before the war, would have been developing gradually in the reserve – or even the third – team. Thanks to conscription, this state of affairs is likely to continue for some time yet. Indeed, I think the situation is likely to take a turn for the worse, before it gets better. For there will come a juncture when the majority of those players with pre-war experience will drop out of the game, and standards will inevitably decline, until those players who have been afforded the full benefit of peace-time training and conditions are ready to take their places.

Let there be no despondency. I do not regard the period in which I played as a golden age, unlikely ever to return. The standards then were high: there is no denying it. But I see no reason at all why British football should not become just as good again, in the future. Today, conscription takes an important period out of the young footballer's early training. True, he received plenty of exercise in the Services, but it is not of a suitable kind. Many people blame British food for recent failures in British sport, and there may be some truth behind this argument. I can only advise the football fan to be patient. In a few years' time he will have his reward.

So much for the present standard of football in Britain. What of the teams and personalities which have been prominent since the war? In season 1947-48 my old club, Arsenal, won the League again. It was a great triumph for Tom Whittaker, in his very first season as Arsenal manager. Shortly after his appointment, in May 1947, he complained to me: "The trouble is, Cliff, that they'll expect me to do what Mr. Chapman did: put Arsenal on top of the League again."

"Don't worry, Tom," I reassured him. "It won't need a very good team to do that."

As things transpired, it didn't. Arsenal cantered away with the Championship, heading the table from the first week of the season, right through until the very end. They were a reasonably good team, and, since I anticipated that any reasonably good team would carry all before it that season, I was not surprised when they did so well. There was no question about the fact that their triumph was well deserved; for, to my mind, they were undoubtedly the best team in the League. But I don't think they bore much comparison with the old Arsenal: and neither did anybody else.

The team which has received the most plaudits, since the end of the war, is Manchester United. Personally, I consider that they have been very much over-praised, although there is no denying that their post-war record is an impressive one. They have adopted the old Corinthians five-in-a-line style of forward play, and the clever pattern-weaving, and crisp inter-passing which this involves had been missing for so long that the thankful sporting journalists swooped on it with an overdose of superlatives. The latter half of the 1947-48 season, when it is generally agreed that the United reached their best, showed them as an unbalanced rather than a brilliant team. There forward line was certainly quite a good one, but the defence was decidedly shaky, and I thought them lucky to beat Blackpool, just an ordinary team, in the Cup Final. Blackpool should never have allowed the United to come from behind, in the way they did.

Perhaps the best post-war eleven has been Portsmouth, a team which thoroughly deserved its first League Championship. Pompey play with immense confidence, and I particularly like the way in which every member of the side tries to use the ball, instead of merely kicking hard, and hoping for the best. They had one of the best ever chances to accomplish the coveted Cup and League double, in 1949, but frittered it away by an inept performance in the Semi-Final, against Second Division Leicester City. Nine times out of ten they would have won this match. Leicester fought with magnificent spirit, but they were an undistinguished side. Portsmouth should never have allowed them to get to Wembley.

There have been a number of footballing personalities since the end of the war. Prominent among them has been Billy Wright, the flaxen-headed captain of England and the Wolves. Billy is a sound tackler and a good constructive player, and there is no denying that he is outstanding among present-day wing half-backs. Good as he is, however, I think he has been a little overrated. I may cause a storm when I say that, in my opinion, he would not have made the England team before the war.

Stanley Mortensen is another player who has distinguished himself. I played many times with Stanley, when he turned out for Arsenal as a guest, during the war. Although his form has been undermined somewhat by ankle injuries, at his best he possesses great speed and dash, together with a powerful shot. Personally I think he is played out of place as an inside-forward. He is essentially an individualist, and is inclined to hold the ball too long, thus poaching on the preserves of his centre-forward. For my own part, I consider Stanley is a centre-forward, or nothing at all.

Other players now well to the fore are Billy Steel of Derby County, who for a few brief months was the world's most expensive footballer; Willy Waddell of Glasgow Rangers and Jimmy Mason of Third Lanark, who have done so well as Scotland's right-wing pair; hard-shooting Billy Liddell, of Liverpool, and Stoke City's cultured Neil Franklin. All are good players. None, by pre-war standards, is great.

What of the politics of present-day football? Personally, I consider the game is in a healthy state. If I had a talented footballing son, instead of two bonny daughters, I would have no hesitation in advising him to go into the professional game: that is, providing he did not already possess a promising future, outside football. But there are undeniably many current problems, and here, for what they are worth, I will give my views on a few of them.

The transfer question at once springs to mind. On the face of it, fantastic fees are being paid for footballers. The £14,000 Arsenal paid for Bryn Jones, in 1938, is now a landmark that has receded far into the dim distance. I myself am inclined to think that present day transfer fees are being viewed disproportionately. That is to say, people are not taking into consideration the phenomenal rise of the cost of living. They willingly pay three times as much as they did before the war for a new suit, but when a football club pays a three times larger sum for a new player, they lift their eyebrows in horror and bewilderment. "But how can a footballer possibly be worth so much?" they plaintively enquire. "How can your suits be so much more expensive?" is the question I would put to them, in an endeavour to answer their own.

Apart from the general rise in prices, two other factors are at the bottom of the present vast size of transfer fees. One, of course, is the dearth of young players, which results in intensive competition for the relatively few stars there are: in fact our old friend, the Law of Supply and Demand. More important, in my opinion, is the extent of the Entertainment and Profits Taxes which the clubs are obliged to pay. Mr. Hugh Dalton did reduce them in 1945, it is true, but the taxes still remained absurdly high. Consequently, when a club makes a large profit, it is faced with the alternative of spending it on its own selfish behalf, or making a fine, public-spirited gift of it to the nation. In the words of the late Sid Walker, "What would you do, chums?" I can tell you what the clubs do. They spend the money on transfer fees, and charge it up to expenses. Can you blame them?

The transfer problem, such as it is, will only resolve itself when the Entertainment and Profit Taxes are appreciably lowered and – though this, as I have said before, is a secondary reason – when good young players become plentiful again.

These large fees definitely have their evils. The greatest of these is that the unfortunate player with a £20,000 label tied round his neck regards it as just that. One can sympathise with him. It would take something of a mental contortion for him to say to himself, "Now, the value of the pound is today roughly one-third of what it was before the war, and therefore I am only worth £6,666." It is made all the more difficult, when the supporters of the new club and the football public at large look at a £20,000 fee from the pre-war standpoint.

Should the player receive a proportion of his transfer fee? is a question which has been very much asked recently. An emphatic no is my answer. For one thing, I do not think that many people realise that a player, when he is transferred, receives his accrued benefit to date, besides his admittedly paltry £10 signing-on fee. The accrued benefit usually amounts to quite a useful sum. Further, the player who is loyal to one club throughout his career would be most unjustly situated, if those transferred were rewarded with proportions of the fees paid for them. Take my own case. Arsenal would almost certainly have refused to transfer me, even if I had requested to go. Yet, say, a reserve player might be allowed to leave Highbury, and would benefit by several hundred pounds. I, on the other hand, would get nothing.

One last word on the subject of transfers. Suggestions have been made that a limit should be placed upon transfer fees. A brief moment's thought should convince the suggesters of the futility of their idea. Its only effect, as I see it, would be to place an overwhelming temptation in the way of the clubs, to falsify their balance sheets. Arbitrary and artificial controls are almost invariably unwise.

Another bone of contention these days is the subject of the payment of players. I fully agree with the general view, and with the Players' Union, that they should receive more. I thoroughly disagree that one man should get more than another. One hears a great deal of facile talk about merit gaining its just reward. I think I can lay fair claim to having attained the top flight, in my own career, but, even so, I strongly maintain that the only effect of unequal payments would be to disrupt team spirit. Football, for better or for worse, is essentially a team game. Only those who have been inside Soccer can understand how easily jealousy can be fomented. It would be only too simple for a highly paid man to be put out of the game by his financially poorer colleagues. And I need hardly emphasise that the greatest of footballers cannot play football without the ball. Forget payment by results, as far as football is concerned. It is a snare and a delusion.

Let us now have a glance at something outside Soccer, but very closely connected with it – the Football Pools. Let us bypass the question of whether they are intrinsically right or wrong. The fact is that they have come to stay, and are making an enormous profit. Britain is not the only country where the Pools hold sway. All over the world, and particularly in Scandinavia, people fill in their ten results, three draws and four aways. The difference is that, in most of these other countries, part at least of the money is taken by the State, and used for the promotion of sport. Why cannot the same be done here? The Pools even went so far as to offer a proportion of their profits to the Football Association, and that august body, with a Victorian shudder of aversion, spurned the tainted offer. It is high time that the ostrich of Lancaster Gate took its head out of the sand.

There are many different, useful ways in which the money from the Pools could be turned to account. The training of young players at once springs to mind. Rapid advances are certainly being made in this country, but much still remains to be done. A second use for the money would be the setting-up of a players' relief fund. I know that one exists already, but I am quite sure that the compensation which it gives out is almost always inadequate. The young International, for example, might, before he is put out of the game by injury, make a great deal of money from sources outside football: by advertising mustard and hair-oil, for example. Of course, it would not always be easy to decide which really were the hard cases, and which were not. Many players who applied would probably have come down in the world through their own failings, rather than through the buffets of Fortune. A joint committee of representatives from the Football Association, the Football League and the Players' Union could act as judges.

Finally, why cannot the Football Association – and the Scottish Association, and the Welsh Association, and the Irish Association, for that matter – afford to pay its International players more than a paltry £20 per match? This, admittedly, is an increase on the payment made before the war, but more should certainly be given. If these associations find it beyond their monetary capacity, may I refer them to my panacea: the Pools? And if a footballer is injured in one International match, so he is forced by that injury to miss the next, the country he was playing for should pay him a full fee, for the International match or matches which he misses. Where is the money to come from: yes, you've guessed it: the Pools!

Next, a few brief words on the subject of the part-time footballer would not be out of place. One famous manager has gone so far as to suggest that only two days of training every week are necessary. Judging by the performances of his team, whenever I see them, he has put his ideas into practice. Football is a full-time job. Played properly, it will never be anything else. The footballer cannot serve two masters. If he takes a job outside the game during the season, his play cannot help but suffer in consequence.

Let me end with a few words on the international expansion of football. Fifty years ago, the game was hardly known outside Britain. Today, South America is football-minded enough to put on the World Cup; English touring teams play in lands as far apart as Brazil and Turkey, Iceland and Spain. Gradually and inevitably, the basis of competitive football will become more and more international. I feel that a start could, and should, be made, with the institution of a European international league.

The British International Championship has lost all its significance. During my own career, Wales were always a good – and sometimes a brilliant – team, while the Irish were usually able to give a reasonable account of themselves. In no less than three of the four matches I played against Wales I finished on the losing side, and four times in the seven seasons which preceded the war did the Principality carry off the Championship, look you! Today, it is a different story. Wales have lost their guiding genius, Secretary Ted Robbins, and without him they will never be the same again. For thirty-six years he inspired Welsh football. Indeed, I would go farther, and say that Ted Robbins *was* Welsh football.

Ireland, now that Eire has seceded from the British Empire, can no longer call upon players from south of the border. Even with them, she has, since 1945, been hard put to hold her own. Without them, she is hopelessly lost. To let through eight goals at home to Scotland, as she did in 1949, is a performance which manifestly shows her team to be below the necessary standard. What is the point of an International Championship which virtually begins and ends each April, with the match between England and Scotland? Mark my words, dear readers: a European Championship will – indeed, must – take its place.

25
IN RETROSPECT

And so I come to the end of my autobiography. Autobiographies are essentially unsatisfying things. The only kind of person in a really good position to write them is that of the tough old French duellist:

"Do you forgive your enemies, my son?" asked the absolving priest, as he lay on his death-bed.

"I have no enemies, Father," replied the dying Frenchman. "I have killed them all."

Prudence and the law of libel – particularly the latter! – forces the autobiographer to pull his punches, to the point of insipidity. So much could be said that must be left out. So many anecdotes and incidents could be recounted – but so many settlements in and out of court would inevitably accrue!

For all that, I have enjoyed writing my autobiography; and now, I stand at the end of it, looking back over nearly twenty years spent in top-class football. If I had my time over again, I would not want to change it. As a professional footballer, I met people and visited countries which I surely would not have done otherwise. France, Germany, Austria, Switzerland, Italy, Hungary – and other lands, besides – flung their gates open for me, thanks to my ability to kick a football about rather better than the next man.

I found professional Soccer a grand life. But it, like everything else, had its more sombre aspects. Although, as I have pointed out, earlier in the book, I was seldom affected by the big occasion, I was nevertheless inclined to worry, whenever I found myself in a bad patch. Sleepless nights do not lead to better football, and sometimes it would take several weeks of bad football, and nervous strain, before I could recapture my usual form.

Playing for Arsenal was always something of a liability. We at Highbury knew the eyes of the football world were upon us, eager to see the slightest mistake. This was an asset as well as a burden to me, however, for it kept me on my toes, throughout my career.

But for all its worries and disappointments – the depression and sense of powerlessness when you are put out of action by an injury; the embarrassment of feeling the eyes of other people on you, when you walk abroad; the constant watch on your diet, and the stupid curiosity of other people when you drink an occasional pint of beer, or smoke an isolated cigarette – Soccer can be a wonderful career. Certainly, I found it so. And as I walked off the field, and down the tunnel that led to the dressing-rooms, after I knew I had played a good game; while the spectators cheered until I had disappeared out of sight: then I knew that the game of football was definitely, gloriously, worth the candle.

Today, my wife and I are running a restaurant, in Edgware; while I am also a sports writer, for the *Sunday Pictorial*. Will I return to the game as a manager? It is a question I have often been asked. A little while ago, a fellow-journalist congratulated me on being appointed manager of a certain London Third Division Club – an appointment which I had not even been offered!

In point of fact, it is probable that I will come back to football, in a more intimate capacity than as a journalist: but not unless I can secure an appointment where the manager is given a free hand. Too many managers today are merely the puppets of their directors. I myself would rather have a free hand as manager of a club at ten pounds a week than be a useless, fettered figurehead, at ten thousand a year.

Whether or not I become a manager in the near future, I shall always look back happily on my football career: a career that brought me twenty-one International caps, four from the Football League; five League Championship medals, three for the Cup Final, and another four for the F.A. Charity Shield. I feel that I have had more than my share of good luck, for happy as I am in the possession of these trophies, I am happier and richer still in the memories which they conjure up.

ALSO AVAILABLE FROM
GCR BOOKS

THE ARSENAL STADIUM MYSTERY
by
LEONARD R. GRIBBLE

A well-known amateur footballer drops dead shortly after half-time in a match between Arsenal Football Club and top amateur side The Trojans in front of 70,000 spectators— every one a witness to murder.

Inspector Anthony Slade of Scotland Yard arrives at the Arsenal Stadium to investigate……

"Like Arsenal in more recent years, it does the double: while scoring highly for nostalgia, it also holds its own in the suspense stakes."
The Independent on Sunday

Visit **www.gcrbooks.co.uk** for details.

ALSO AVAILABLE FROM
GCR BOOKS

FORWARD, ARSENAL!
by
BERNARD JOY

The first detailed history of Arsenal Football Club covering the period from the Club's humble origins in Woolwich in 1886; the move to Highbury in 1913; the successful decade of the 1930's under the guidance of Herbert Chapman and George Allison; the post-war period under Tom Whittaker and ending with an account of the title-winning season 1952-3.

"This is a magnificent book.......... If you are serious about supporting Arsenal, about knowing Arsenal's history, and about venerating our past as well as our present, you need this". **Untold Arsenal**

Visit **www.gcrbooks.co.uk** for details.

ALSO AVAILABLE FROM
GCR BOOKS

FOOTBALL AMBASSADOR
by
EDDIE HAPGOOD

Football Ambassador was the first football autobiography and was written at the end of a long and successful career during which the author played 440 games for Arsenal and gained 43 England caps.

Hapgood tells the story of his career, introduces the great players of his era and recounts his experiences with Arsenal and England with both honesty and a touch of humour.

".....*memorable account of life at Highbury during the club's golden inter-war period.*" **Jem Maidment, Ham & High**

Visit **www.gcrbooks.co.uk** for details.

ALSO AVAILABLE FROM
GCR BOOKS

HERBERT CHAPMAN
on
FOOTBALL

The reflections of Arsenal's Greatest Manager

Herbert Chapman entered into football management by accident. Everything he did thereafter was pure genius. Light years ahead of his time Chapman was to revolutionise professional football and the sport as an entertainment industry.

Chapman's ideas were visionary but many took years to be accepted by the Football Association. He advocated numbered shirts, white footballs, the ten-yard semi-circle, floodlit matches, goal-judges, better refereeing and a plan for improving the England team.

Within five years of his arrival at Arsenal, Chapman created a team that was to dominate English football for a decade.

Herbert Chapman on Football is an accumulation of articles Chapman wrote for *The Sunday Express*. It was first published after his premature death in 1934.

Visit **www.gcrbooks.co.uk** for details.

ALSO AVAILABLE FROM
GCR BOOKS

BILLY GOONER'S FIRST MATCH
by
GREG ADAMS

Billy Gooner's First Match is a story about a special occasion for all Arsenal supporters; going to watch the team play for the very first time.

It's 1976 and Billy Gooner celebrates his seventh birthday with an unexpected trip to Highbury with his Dad to watch Arsenal play West Ham United.

Billy's day is filled with highs and lows and lots of goals and ends with a birthday surprise he'll treasure forever.

Visit **www.gcrbooks.co.uk** for details.

ARSENAL INDEPENDENT SUPPORTERS' ASSOCIATION

AISA was formed on Sunday 1st October 2000, hours before Thierry Henry's 'wonder goal' at Highbury that led to a 1-0 victory over Manchester United. Over 50 supporters attended the inaugural meeting at St. Paul's Road, London N1, with most joining up immediately. AISA's membership, including associate members, has since grown to over 8,000, making it by far the largest Arsenal supporters club.

The main objects of **AISA** are to:

- Represent and campaign on behalf of Arsenal supporters.
- Organise high quality services for **AISA** members.
- Promote, maintain and value the history and independence of Arsenal Football Club.
- Encourage the Directors and Management of Arsenal Football Club to appreciate, welcome and value the support and participation of all Arsenal fans.

AISA believes that fans' views and experiences should be at the centre of the Club's decision-making process. We work co-operatively with the Arsenal Supporters' Trust and REDaction, and also have a high regard for The Gooner fanzine and various Arsenal Supporters Clubs, with whom we liaise closely.

AISA campaigns on issues such as improving the atmosphere, providing better catering arrangements, the stewarding and policing operations, transport to and from the stadium. We meet regularly with the Club's chief executive, and with various other Arsenal senior managers and directors.

Everything we do is informed by our members, through their feedback, and by fans in general through regular surveys and various other formal and informal tools.

AISA has developed a charity fundraising programme, mainly supporting the Arsenal charity of the season, which has raised over £65,000 in the last 4 years.
We are opposed to any changes in the ownership of the Club that would lead to a major increase in debt or in securing short-term profits through significant hikes in ticket prices.

AISA has a number of important relationships with external organisations, notably Islington Borough Council and the Islington Police.

Every Arsenal supporter is welcome to join **AISA**. We have members as young as 8 and others well into their 80s. Many members attend matches every week, others are not so lucky but support the team in every way they can. **AISA** is based in Islington but our members live in every part of the UK, and in over 40 other countries.

Membership fees are minimal; join up at www.aisa.org or write to AISA, PO Box 65011, London N5 9AX. For more information email us at info@aisa.org or call 07706 885078.

The Arsenal Supporters' Trust exists to bring together Shareholders and Supporters of Arsenal Football Club.

Our goal is to widen and deepen supporter ownership, representation and influence at Arsenal. Large numbers of our members are already personal Arsenal shareholders.

Every member of the Trust shares in ownership of Arsenal Football Club through the shares the Trust owns.

The Trust works with its members, Arsenal executives, the club's Board, major shareholders and other Arsenal supporter groups to help build Arsenal into a world class sporting institution.

Arsenal is a name and a club already widely admired around the football world. Together we can take it to even greater heights, both on and off the field. The Arsenal tradition is one of ground-breaking innovation. Please join us and support our work.

As well as holding monthly board meetings which members are welcome to attend, the Trust holds special events for its membership. In recent seasons, these have included an annual Q&A session with the managing director/CEO of the club, a Christmas drinks social in Arsenal's exclusive Diamond Club, a tour of the stadium's press facilities and a meeting for members with relevant ministers at the Houses of Parliament.

For details of how to join, visit our website at
www.arsenaltrust.org